THE ROUX BROTHERS ON
· *PATISSERIE* ·

THE ROUX BROTHERS ON
· PATISSERIE ·

MICHEL &
ALBERT ROUX

PHOTOGRAPHS BY ANTHONY BLAKE

LITTLE, BROWN

A LITTLE, BROWN BOOK

First published in Great Britain in 1986
by Macdonald & Co (Publishers) Ltd

This paperback edition first published in 1993 by
Little, Brown and Company

Reprinted 1996 , 2000

British Cataloguing in Publication Data
Roux, Albert
     The Roux brothers on patisserie.
     1. Pastry   2. Cookery, French
     I.Title   II. Roux, Michel
     641.8′65   TX773

ISBN 0-316-90559-3

This book was designed and produced by
QED Publishing Ltd
The Old Brewery, 6 Blundell Street, London N7 9BH

Project Director Alastair Campbell
Translated by Kate and Tessa Rose
Art Editor Moira Clinch

Editorial Director Jim Miles

Illustrations Liza Adamezewski

Typeset by Q V Typesetting, London
Manufactured in Hong Kong by
Regent Publishing Services Limited
Printed by Leefung-Asco Printers Limited,China

Little, Brown and Company (UK)
Brettenham House
Lancaster Place
London
WC2E 7EN

The Publishers would like to thank the many people who
have helped in the preparation of this book, especially the
following: Laura Beck of QV Typesetting; Mr Maghbroda
for the use of his orchard; Osborne & Little and Falkiner
Fine Papers for supplying background papers used in the
book; Sarah Campbell; Dickens & Jones for supplying
picnic hampers. Thanks go to Suzannah Smith of The
Conran Shop, Colin Harris of Wedgwood, Camilla Adams
of General Trading Company (Mayfair) Ltd., Caroline
Franklin of Reject China Shops, Abbie Sinclair of Eli-
zabeth Davis Ltd., and Lynne Stephenson and Jeanette
Gallbraith of Rosenthal for lending the chinaware used in
the photographs. All the kitchen equipment illustrated in
this book can be obtained from Maison Mora, speciality
suppliers of utensils for patisserie, 13 Rue Montmarte
B.P.273, 75024 Paris Codex 01.

To Jean-Louis Berthelot
(1951–1979)

The craftsman, the artist, the friend, whose death was so
untimely; in only a few short years, he brought and bestowed
more knowledge to our craft than most men could have
achieved in fifty years.

Coupe Grand Prix Charles Proust 1971
Médaille d'Or Arpajon 1971
Premier Commis de France 'Cusenier' 1971
Médaille d'Or Académie Culinaire Française 1971
International Gold Medal, Vienna 1974
1st prize: Sèvres vase, given by President Valéry Giscard d'Estaing, 1974
Meilleur Ouvrier de France 1976
Compagnon du Tour de France 1976
Chevalier des Arts, Sciences et Lettres 1977
Culinary Trophy of New York (Chef of the Year 1977)
Chevalier Côteaux de Champagne 1977
Chevaliers Cuiseurs du Sucre 1978

With profound respect, Michel and Albert pay homage to
Jean-Louis

---

*T*he authors would like to express special thanks to all the people listed here,
without whose help this book could never have been written: Robyn Roux, for her
invaluable good sense and loyal support; John Hubert, senior lecturer at the Slough
College of Higher Education, winner of numerous gold and silver medals in
international competitions for patisserie work, chief examiner for advanced pastry
courses (City & Guilds), member of the Académie Culinaire de France, U.K., who
read all the recipes for us; Guy Barbé, chef de partie at The Waterside Inn, who
tested most of the recipes and took part in almost all the photographic sessions;
Geneviève Barbé for typing the manuscript; Moira Clinch and Carolyn King for
their dedication and diligence in designing and editing the book; and finally Kate
Whiteman for her excellent and sympathetic translation.

CONFÉDÉRATION NATIONALE
DE LA
PÂTISSERIE-CONFISERIE-GLACERIE

For many years I have had the very highest regard for the Roux brothers — how could it be otherwise? Here are two men who, throughout their professional lives, have given the best possible service to their employers. Their courage, taste and attention to detail, combined with a love of their craft and hard work, have brought them to the very pinnacle of gastronomic achievement.

Albert is regarded by his peers as one of the greatest chefs in the world, while Michel is recognised as not only a very great chef, but also a master pâtissier — one of the Meilleurs Ouvriers de France in patisserie.

Here are two brothers, as inseparable in private life as they are professionally, who are prepared to face up to any situation, however difficult — look how they left their native land and came to London, speaking not a word of English, to snatch six Michelin stars for their two restaurants.

But they will not stop at that. Aware that honours demand duties, they have decided to share their knowledge and skill by writing two books — the enormously successful New Classic Cuisine, and now The Roux Brothers on Patisserie. You may be sure that professionals and beginners alike will find this book is the definitive guide to the art of patisserie.

I can confirm that this is a book full of riches, both in content and presentation. Its readers will find it an inspiration and from it will learn all there is to know about the noble craft of patisserie.

I offer Albert and Michel my congratulations and thanks on behalf of our profession.

Jean Millet M.O.F.
President

INTRODUCTION

*I*n this book, you will find many recipes, hints and tricks of the trade, gleaned from years of experience, right back to our earliest years in the profession. Our inspiration has come from the exercise books we kept as apprentices, when day after day we scribbled down tips and notes on pages besmeared by our buttery fingers.

Although most of our recipes are classic, we have adapted them to our own taste and to conform with modern ideas. Many of these dishes were once served in the private houses where we worked as chefs; today they appear on the menu at our restaurants, Le Gavroche and The Waterside Inn. We have given the most detailed instructions possible for all the dishes, so that, however simple or complex the recipe may be, it will be easy to follow. To ensure that each recipe is produced to the highest standard, we have limited the number presented in this volume and chosen to omit certain chapters like confectionery, chocolates and fresh, glazed or candied petits fours.

PATISSERIE: PAST AND PRESENT

From time immemorial, children have been attracted to the sweet scents of vanilla, lemon and sugar which their grandmothers and mothers used in their baking.

Waffles, pale, golden brown, topped with whipped cream, *crêpes* filled with jam, warm mirabelle tarts — these fragrant images remain firmly embedded in our memory.

The patisserie of yesterday has not disappeared; all the recipes of our heritage are founded upon it. But perhaps it is time to update it to conform to today's culinary ideas. Certain desserts, like those filled with buttercream or frangipane (mocha and *mascotte* cakes and *mille-feuilles,* for example) are less popular than they used to be. We no longer have the same passion for choux buns, eclairs, *réligieuses* or *Paris-Brest.* Elaborate piped decorations, silver balls and mimosa have declined in popularity, as have gateaux with fondant icing. Pastries and portions of cake, which were often far too large, have become smaller and more delicate. Even ice creams are making way for fresh fruit sorbets.

A *pâtissier* sells a little happiness to children, young people and adults alike, but nowadays he dispenses a healthier bounty. His confections contain less

Michel Roux's apprenticeship was served under the searching gaze of M Camille Loyal,
pictured here with his wife outside his patisserie in the Paris district of Belleville in 1956.

butter and sugar and fewer eggs than they did twenty years ago and, as a result, his cakes are so light that we can enjoy them at any time of day, even when we aren't particularly hungry. There is no doubt that, eaten in moderation, butter, sugar and eggs are vital to our well-being.

The past few years have seen a very important change in our approach to desserts; elaborate decorations, too, have been much simplified and, indeed, have almost disappeared. Now, charlottes with fruit *coulis* abound — what is more divine than a pear charlotte? Bitter chocolate is often the main ingredient in a pudding, and in patisserie fruits (often exotic) reign supreme; they are pure and natural and offer an endless range of possibilities — *bavaroises, bombes,* charlottes, mousses, ice creams and tarts. It is a pity, though, that the ubiquitous kiwi fruit has become somewhat over-used, both in savoury dishes and in patisserie.

Fruit sorbets, too, are much in demand, adding a magical, refreshing note to the end of a meal. Mousses, alas, are now so commonplace that many people are becoming bored with them.

Obviously, it is easier to create really original patisserie at home or in a restaurant than in a shop. The restaurateur is fortunate because he can prepare the most delicate and fragile desserts which have only to be carried from kitchen to dining room and not from shop to home. Thus he can offer his famous *assiette du chef* — a plateful of tiny portions of his most sumptuous desserts — and set it all before a dumbfounded and amazed gourmet, who can scarcely take in such a feast for eye and palate.

THE SEMINAR FOR THE MAITRES PATISSIERS OF FRANCE

Every year, Michel takes part in the seminar of the *Maîtres Pâtissiers de France*. Sixty or so master *pâtissiers*, aged between 30 and 65, gather together for this gastronomic happening with its three days of culinary demonstrations. Among their number are found the most famous *pâtissiers* of France and between them they own the finest patisseries in the land.

From six o'clock in the morning till six at night, they assemble in groups of six to eight, and for two to three hours each *pâtissier* demonstrates his art to the rest of the assembled company.

The last morning of this seminar is spent discussing and debating the ground covered during the first two days. New ideas and methods are approved or rejected; problems are aired and solutions suggested. Thus, the whole future of patisserie in France is shaped. Our profession can only evolve for the better if experts like these are prepared to share all their secrets.

BECOMING A MEILLEUR OUVRIER DE FRANCE

France's most prestigious competition is organised by the state every three years. It brings together representatives from 217 professions, assembled in 17 groups, including mosaics, ironmongery, sculpture, floral art, culinary art — all trades where hand and mind combine.

The title of 'Meilleur Ouvrier' was officially recognized by a decree which appeared in the official trades journal no. 194 on 21 August 1980. It was classed as equivalent to Level 4 in education: Technical *Baccalauréat*, Certificate of Mastership, etc. In other words, it entitles the holder to teach at the highest technical level.

Once the participants have enrolled for the competition, they are given the subject matter and size of the piece they must create. The general commissioner or his deputies oversee and control the work in progress. First, a departmental jury judges the quality of the work; if it meets with their

MEILLEUR OUVRIER DE FRANCE

My body trembles as though I have been beaten, my throat is tight with emotion, my eyes brim with tears — they have just announced my name; my work as a pâtissier-confiseur has received the ultimate recognition and I have been honoured with the title of 'un des Meilleurs Ouvriers de France 1976, Pâtissier-Confiseur'; in other words, I am considered to be one of France's finest craftsmen in pâtisserie. Drained by the physical effort of the hundreds of hours of work and the nervous tension of the past few weeks, I hardly dare believe it. All I know is that I am here and I have succeeded. I stagger, I lurch forward as though in a dream to collect that gold medal on its red, white and blue ribbon, the first to be presented by the President of the French Republic, Monsieur Valéry Giscard d'Estaing.

I am burning hot. I am consumed by that fire which burns in every craftsman who cares passionately about his work. This is the strongest emotion I have ever felt in all my thirty-five years. I feel intoxicated. My mind flashes back, as in a film, to the master whose apprentice I was, who awoke in the adolescent I was then that most precious love for this work. I can see the craftsmen who guided me, my colleagues and my friends, the MOFs who gave me good advice — I see everyone who has helped to teach me my wonderful craft. To them I give my joy, my pride and my gratitude.

THE GLITTERING PRIZE

After many years of sheer hard work and single-minded dedication came public recognition with the award of the gold medal and the title 'Meilleur Ouvrier de France'. Some of the pieces, made in the course of the competition, that won Michel Roux the coveted title include:

ABOVE *Chocolate presentation, made completely out of chocolate — both dark and white — and accompanied by six varieties of chocolates, has a contemporary flavour.*

ABOVE *The pièce de résistance — 'A window opening onto Spring'. The view through the open window is in pastillage, hand-painted with edible food colouring, as are the balcony and window frame. The window glazing is formed from Sucre coulé. The exuberant vine with its glossy flowers and leaves is made from Sucre tiré. It took more than 70 hours to create this particular piece.*

LEFT *Six different petits fours frais, presented on individual hand-painted pastillage bases.*

approval, it is then presented to the national juries. But now let Michel take up the story.

'On Monday 6 September 1976, I came to the final in which I was participating. Only twenty candidates had been short-listed. They came from everywhere – Paris, the provinces, even, like me, from abroad. The theme for our artistic presentation was "Spring"; I decided to christen mine "A window opening onto Spring". First there was to be a dessert designed for a baptism, then six sorts of glazed petits fours and six kinds of chocolates. We also had to model from sugar any flowers, fruits or animals of our choice. Our aim was to surpass ourselves, to scale new heights of excellence in pastry-making, dessert-creating, in preparing little cakes and vast cakes for catering – in short, in every aspect of the craft, we aimed to be complete masters of our art. To crown it all, we had to create pieces for special occasions and ceremonies, designed to titillate the palate and satisfy the most demanding of clients.

'Obviously, it is not possible to classify all the various crafts in the competition all together. That is why every three years a total of 400 craftsmen, representing every trade, are chosen from tens of thousands of hopeful competitors to become MOFs. In my year, seven *pâtissiers-confiseurs* were awarded the title of "un des Meilleurs Ouvriers de France" and I am happy to give you all their names. They are, from left to right: M Jean-Louis Berthelot, from La Celle-Saint-Cloud; M Gérard Hee, from Paris; M Michel Foussard, from Paris; M Gérard Moyne-Bressand, from Nîmes; M G. Marzet (President); M Yves Thuries, from Gaillac; M René Fontaine, from Langeac; and myself.'

USING THIS BOOK

*T*his most important part of the book can and should be consulted at all times. It is intended to teach and give simple guidance, and to remind you of certain facts and guidelines which you may have forgotten.

It is easy enough for a *pâtissier* to divulge his recipes, but a great deal harder to teach his skills and techniques in a book, for they have become second nature to him. It is these techniques which make all the difference to a creative piece of patisserie, which raise it from attractive to stunning, from good to excellent, and make it a source of pride.

· THE GOLDEN RULES ·

There are three vital ground rules for following a recipe successfully:

1 Have ready to hand all the equipment you will need for the recipe.
2 Weigh out and measure all the ingredients before commencing the recipe.
3 Preheat the oven to the desired temperature.
By following these golden rules you will find you can produce desserts and pastries easily and quickly.

Before embarking on the recipes in this book, there are some important points you should note.

· MEASUREMENTS ·

All our recipes have been tested using metric measurements and, if possible, you should use these precise measurements. For perfect results it is worth investing in a set of metric measuring spoons, jug and scales. If you feel you have to use the imperial system, bear in mind that these quantities can not be as specific as the metric scale. Imperial measurements in this book have been rounded up or down to the nearest half-ounce and half-fluid ounce. Whichever system you choose, stick to it; do not mix metric and imperial measures in one recipe. Conversion tables are given on page 245.

· INGREDIENTS ·

In order to achieve a perfect result in patisserie, basic ingredients such as butter, eggs and cream must be ultra-fresh and of the finest quality.

One or two ingredients can be difficult to find in local shops and alternatives may be substituted. For example, we use gelatine leaves each weighing 3 g/$\frac{1}{10}$ oz approximately, but these can be replaced by the same weight of powdered gelatine; *couverture* can be replaced by best quality, plain chocolate cake covering. Unless otherwise specified, all butter in the recipes is unsalted; sugar is caster sugar; flour is sifted plain flour.

The preparation time given for each recipe begins after all the ingredients have been weighed and measured, and all the necessary equipment is ready to hand.

Recommended storage times are for food kept in an airtight container or wrapped or covered in clingfilm.

· EQUIPMENT ·

The flan ring and mould sizes given in the recipes are ideal dimensions. Your own existing equipment should, if used, approximate the specified measurements.

Where a copper pan or casserole is given, you can use a heavy, copper-bottomed stainless steel pan instead.

· OVEN TEMPERATURES ·

These tend to vary from oven to oven so we suggest you use an oven thermometer. The results achieved in baking can vary according to the oven. On the whole, domestic gas ovens do not reach such high temperatures as commercial ovens and for this reason we have quoted slightly higher gas conversions than those generally given.

It is very important to watch cakes carefully during baking and not to place too much faith in the temperature indicated by the thermostat but rely instead on a cooking thermometer.

°C	°F	Gas	°C	°F	Gas
100	200	¼	180	350	5
110	225	¼	190	375	6
120	240	½	200	400	7
130	250	1	220	425	8
140	275	2	230	450	9
150	300	3	240	475	10
170	325	4	250	500	10

· SERVING TEMPERATURE ·

All patisserie must be served at the temperature which best suits its flavour and texture. This is why we have never used a sweet trolley at Le Gavroche and The Waterside Inn. All our desserts are kept in the kitchen at the correct temperature and are served to order, with no risk of being spoilt through careless cutting or inept serving by a waiter who is not a highly qualified *pâtissier*.

Chocolate-based desserts: mousses, *ganaches*, etc.	6°-8°C/42°-48°F
Fruit mousse-based desserts: charlottes, etc.	8°-12°C/48°-52°F
Warm puddings, such as tarts and some *feuilletés*.	35°-45°C/95°-104°F
Hot puddings, mainly soufflés.	Between 70° and 80°C/158° and 176°F

PRACTICAL ADVICE ON
· METHODS AND TECHNIQUES ·

Almond paste or marzipan: If it is crumbly or too firm, soften with fondant or glucose.

Coffee: Ground coffee will keep its flavour if it is stored in an airtight container in the fridge.

Fondant: When you warm it, add some 30° Baumé sorbet syrup and a little nut of glucose to soften the

fondant and make it glossy. Never add uncooked egg whites, as they might cause the fondant to ferment; health regulations forbid the addition of raw egg whites.

To beat: Always do this with a whisk.

To grease or butter: Use softened, clarified or melted butter as appropriate. It is important to use precisely the right quantity of butter for greasing moulds, flan rings, baking sheets, etc. Too much butter may crinkle the pastry; not enough may cause the food to stick. You can also buy a silicone spray, which eliminates the need for greasing.

To incorporate: Fold in with a flat slotted spoon, spatula or whisk.

To line: Do this with flour, sugar, ice cream or jelly etc, always using the exact quantity — neither too much nor too little.

To mix: Always do this with a spatula, paddle or whisk.

Sifting: This is necessary to get rid of any foreign particles and lumps in powdery ingredients such as flour, baking powder, ground almonds, cocoa, etc. It also aerates them. Flour must always be sifted for all pastry work.

Flouring: This prevents the dough from sticking to the marble or wooden surface and makes rolling out easier. Sprinkle the flour in a fine cloud, a very little at a time, and brush away any excess before lining a dish with the pastry or placing it on a baking sheet.

Working with dough: Dough taken from the freezer must be left at 5°C/41°F for several hours to allow it to thaw gradually before using.

Maximum kneading of leavened dough or puff pastry: The dough is sufficiently kneaded when all the ingredients are incorporated and, after the dough has been kneaded for some time, the ball of dough comes cleanly away from the sides of the bowl or work surface. By this time, the flour will have absorbed all the moisture, and the dough will be elastic.

Rising of doughs leavened with yeast: If you are kneading dough in a warm temperature, chill the liquid ingredients (eggs, milk and water) before using. The temperature of the dough after kneading should never exceed 24°C/75°F.

After rich yeast-leavened doughs (eg, croissants, *brioches*, Viennese pastries, etc) have fermented in a warm place, it is best to leave them to 'relax' at room temperature for a further 15 minutes before baking so that they develop a full, even spring and puff up as much as possible during cooking.

Storing all types of uncooked dough: Before placing in the fridge, wrap the dough in polythene to prevent it from drying out and forming a crust.

Refrigerating puff pastry: Puff pastry must be brought to room temperature before using, so that the fat content has time to soften. If the pastry is too cold, the layers of fat might break during rolling and the dough will not develop and rise fully.

Rolled-out pastry: Move this by rolling it loosely onto a rolling pin, so as not to spoil the shape or break it. This applies to puff pastry, almond paste, etc.

Lining: To prevent the pastry from shrinking during cooking, line the mould the day before if possible and keep in the fridge or freezer. In any event, the pastry must be left to rest for at least an hour before baking.

Allow about 50 g/2 oz pastry per person when making a tart or flan case.

Puff pastry: Place the rolled-out dough on a baking sheet dampened with water. This will prevent the pastry from slipping when you glaze it and stops it from shrinking during cooking, which would spoil the shape.

Staggered rows: Always arrange all pastry tins, tartlet and *brioche* moulds, etc. in staggered rows on the baking sheet to ensure more even cooking.

Glazing with eggwash: For a really shiny finish, it is best to give two light coats of glaze. A single, heavier glaze is more likely to run.

To make a durable glaze for puff pastry desserts (eg, Pithiviers,): Sprinkle with icing sugar at the end of cooking, and place in a very hot oven for a few moments to obtain a subtle, varnish-like glaze. If you use a 30° Baumé sorbet syrup to glaze, it may become dull and whitish after several hours, as the sugar recrystallises.

Egg yolks: These 'burn' when they come into contact with sugar or salt, so they must be beaten immediately with a whisk or spatula until completely homogenous. If this is not done, hard little granules of yolk will form, and it is impossible to get rid of them.

Stiffly beaten egg whites: To ensure that egg whites rise perfectly, all utensils must be scrupulously clean. Rinse them in cold water and allow to dry thoroughly before using.

Make sure that there is no trace of yolk left in the whites.

If they are very fresh, add a pinch of salt to break them down. Start by beating the whites at medium speed to make them frothy, and stretch them as much as possible, then increase the speed to high to firm them up.

When flecks of beaten egg white appear at the edges of the bowl, add a little sugar to prevent them from becoming grainy. They will be firmer and easier to mix and handle. This is very important in both savoury and sweet soufflés.

Weighing eggs:
Size 1   at least 70 g/2½ oz.
Size 2   65-70 g/2¼-2½ oz.
Size 3   60-65 g/2-2¼ oz.
Size 4   55-60 g/2 oz approx.
Size 5   50-55 g/1 ¾ oz approx.
Size 6   45-50 g/1½-1¾ oz.
Size 7   under 45 g/1½ oz.

A medium egg weighing about 60 g/2 oz contains approximately 30 g/1 oz white; 20 g/¾ oz yolk; 10 g/¼ oz shell.

20 whole eggs = 1 L/1 ¾ pts
32 egg whites = 1 L/1¾ pts
52 egg yolks = 1 L/1¾ pts

Freezing egg whites: Freeze them just as they are; they will keep very well for several weeks.

Freezing yolks: Beat them lightly with 5-10 per cent sugar, then freeze at -25°C/-13°F for not more than four weeks.

Cold storage: Modern methods of cold storage have opened up new horizons and make for more efficient methods of working.

Fridge: 5°C/41°F.

'Holding' freezer: -18°C/0°F.

Freezer: -25°C/-13°F.

Blast freezer: -35°C/-31°F. (Ideally, you should freeze food for 30 minutes at this temperature before transferring it to the 'holding' freezer.)

Making nougatine: In humid weather, add 50 g/2 oz butter or fat for each 1 kg/2 lb 2 oz as soon as you have mixed in the almonds; this will prevent the *nougatine* from attracting surface moisture.

Hygiene: One final general observation; we strongly recommend that you wear neither a watch nor jewellery when making patisserie. They can cause allergies and, because there is a tendency for flour and icing to get into the crevices, they are unhygienic.

CHAPTER
· 1 ·

THE BASIC
MATERIALS

Nowadays we tend to forget that the basic ingredients for patisserie were once produced by the *pâtissiers* themselves in the slack periods between the festive seasons. Only thirty years ago, one *pâtissier* in two in every town (more in country areas) skinned the almonds himself and from them made his own *tant pour tant, praliné* and marzipan. He would also make simple fondant icing and maybe prepare his own apple fillings.

Nothing can be nicer for an apprentice (as we were in those days) than to help in the making of hazelnut or almond *praliné*. How greedily we enjoyed watching and smelling the pounding of the nuts!

Today, all these basic ingredients are manufactured in factories; this ensures tighter health controls, consistently high quality and better keeping qualities. Professional and amateur *pâtissiers* can now obtain at any time of year whatever ingredients they need for every conceivable type of patisserie.

Kitchen equipment must be chosen with care and should always be top quality. Buy it from long-established specialist suppliers; their research departments consult professional chefs about their needs before launching new products on the market, so you can be assured that the equipment they sell will be useful, efficient and durable.

Good quality equipment is essential if you are to produce successful dishes. Quantity is far less important and this is why we have classified the equipment in three categories. The first short but adequate list allows the beginner to take his first faltering steps without spending a fortune or making expensive mistakes; this equipment will suffice for most of our recipes.

The second is a complementary list for the more experienced cook, and the third list is intended for professional chefs and amateur patisserie fanatics.

We have used non-stick baking parchment or silicone paper for several years now; it is easy to peel off and does away with the need for greasing. Metal flan rings ensure more even cooking and lift off neatly for easy unmoulding. Bake tarts or flans directly on a baking sheet inside a flan ring. These flan rings are also useful for Genoise sponges, sponge biscuits etc.

If you do not possess a flan ring, you can easily make one from a strip of cardboard cut to the desired length and depth. Stick the ends with sellotape and cover the ring with strips of greaseproof paper or foil. This type of ring is fine for assembling desserts, but not, of course, for cooking them!

Soufflés will rise best if you cook them in a bain-marie or on a baking sheet which has been preheated for ten minutes.

Brioches too will develop much better during cooking if baked on a preheated baking sheet.

Always soak a new pastry brush in lukewarm water for twenty-four hours before using it to prevent it from shedding its hairs. Small kitchen utensils should be washed in hot water and detergent but rinsed in cold; this will achieve a form of sterilization.

When sizes for flan rings, cake boards and other equipment are specified in a recipe, these are only approximate; there is no need to abandon a recipe because you do not possess a utensil of the precise size given!

A GRAIN OF SALT, A GRAIN OF SUGAR

Fundamentally, these two ingredients are diametrically opposed, both in their basic properties and in the way we use them. And yet, they stand together in the dock, each accused of the same crime — that of 'endangering health'.

Faddishness, snobbery, defenders of the steady march towards healthy living, be they dieticians or even cooks — they have all found not one, but both of them, guilty.

Used in moderation, however, these ingredients are essential to a balanced diet and our physical well-being. For generations, they have been a means of survival in times when food was in short supply. They are natural agents which highlight flavours, sweeten dishes and heighten colours, as well as preserving and conserving foodstuffs. Patisserie, like all cookery, would be lost without them; they are essential to life the world over, no matter what the climate, race, religion or lifestyle.

As for us, nothing will change our natural tastes and needs, so let us all cherish 'a grain of salt, a grain of sugar'.

· ESSENTIAL EQUIPMENT ·

1 *Plastic scraper*
2 *Pastry crimper*
3 *Dough scissors*
4 *Vegetable peeler*
5 *Apple corer*
6 *Small sharp knife*
7 *Filleting knife*
8 *Serrated knife*
9 *Three sizes of flexible knife with supple, stainless steel blade. Buy the best quality knives for the best*

result and the longest lifespan. Always dry the knife blade as soon as it is washed.
10 *Flat, wooden-handled pastry brush.*
11 *Two wooden spatulas. Remember not to leave these in any cooking preparation as they will absorb the flavour and then impart this taste to the next sauce or cream that you prepare. Use*

them for stirring and then rest them on top of the saucepan.

<u>RIGHT</u>
1 *A family-sized, electric ice cream machine is a worthwhile investment which will pay for itself in any ice cream- or sorbet-loving family. Ice creams and sorbets are inexpensive to make, particularly*

if seasonal fruits are incorporated.
2 *Balloon whisk*
3 *Dough hook*
4 *Electric mixer with plastic paddle. This is indispensible. Choose the best quality and the most dependable make; it should last a lifetime.*
5 *A splash-guard prevents dry ingredients such as icing sugar from blowing about.*

ABOVE

1 Conical strainer
2 Rubber scraper
3 Wooden spatula
4 Ladle
5 Automatic weighing scales
6 Piping bag
7 A variable-gauge rolling pin. By changing the end rings you can control the thickness of the pastry — an invention which makes rolling pastry to a predetermined thickness foolproof.
8 A revolving turntable makes decorating a large cake with a piping bag or paper cornet easy.
9 Flour or sugar dredger
10 Set of fluted pastry cutters
11 Set of plain round pastry cutters
12 Measuring jug
13 Piping nozzles
14 Fruit press

15 Skimmer or flat slotted spoon
16 Fine mesh metal strainer
17 Flouring brush
18 Double mesh wooden sieves, size 40 for icing sugar, size 25 for flour, size 16 for ground almonds. It is best to avoid washing these sieves; dust with a dry brush after each use.

· ESSENTIAL EQUIPMENT ·

1 Round-bottomed stainless steel mixing bowl is an ideal shape for any process involving a whisk.
2 Wire whisk for sauces and creams
3 Tray for small madeleines
4 Large fluted brioche mould
5 Tuile-shaper tray
6 Flat-bottomed stainless steel mixing bowl
7 Flan ring
8 Round sponge biscuit rings are available in sizes from about 5-30 cm/2-12 in and in rectangular and square shapes as well. It is more popular than any other sponge or biscuit mould.
9 Plain round tartlet tin
10 Small fluted brioche mould

RIGHT

Essences are very useful to give a boost of flavour to a natural ingredient. The best quality essence is made from the natural extract. The flavour must be discreet and not overpower the taste of the preparation so use sparingly. Once opened, the essence will last 6-12 months and will lose some of its strength.
1 Vanilla, **2** Coffee, **3** Orange blossom water, **4** Lemon zest, **5** Pistachio, **6** Bitter almond, **7** Orange.

1 *Wire rack*
2 *Baking sheet*
3 *Non-stick baking parchment*
4 *Silicone paper for baking can be re-used about 30 times. It is one of the most important new introductions to small equipment in pastry. The surface is extremely smooth, giving a perfect finish to cake, dough or pastry. No ingredient will stick to it.*
5 *Soufflé dish*
6 *Rectangular tin with sliding lid*
7 *Saucepans*
8 *Crêpe or pancake pan*
9 *Black metal baking sheet — an ideal shape and size for cooking a single tart.*

· ADVANCED EQUIPMENT ·

1 *A rigid conical strainer is mainly for draining fruits in syrup, and for straining sauces or fruit coulis which are quite thick.*
2 *Large plain savarin mould*
3 *Baking mould for bûche de Noël or tuile shaper*
4 *Small baba mould with a rim*
5 *Small savarin mould*
6 *Small plain barquette tin*
7 *Blinis pan*
8 *Large round brioche or mousseline mould which could be substituted by a small, high-sided, -ovenproof saucepan.*
9 *Stainless steel wire rack*
10 *Stainless steel baba drainer*
11 *Large lined copper Tart Tatin*

mould. Without a handle, it takes up less room in the oven.
12 *Round colander with feet*
13 *Icing tray with grill*

<u>RIGHT</u>
Basic food colourings are used primarily for decorating marzipan, royal icing, pastillage, etc. The decorative elements are, of course, more for visual effect and are certainly not consumed in any quantity. For pastry preparation they are not essential; it is better to retain the colour of the natural ingredients. It is not necessary to buy the entire range of colourings. You can blend your own with a

selection of primary and secondary colours: **1** *Green,* **2** *Blue,* **3** *Yellow,* **4** *Black, and* **5** *Red. Powdered food colourings are much stronger than liquid, dissolving easily in a few drops of water. For colouring sugar, dissolve it in 90° proof alcohol or Cognac which will evaporate during cooking.*

ABOVE

1 Glazing iron for Crème brulée, Crème Chiboust, etc must be heated to very hot in either a gas flame or the coals of a fire. A more sophisticated electric model is available.

2 Sugar thermometer

3 Wooden rolling pin for pastry

4 Metal pastry scraper and cutter

5 Copper sugar pan

6 This small decorating comb is very effective for mixing dark and white couverture for making 2-tone chocolate curls (see page 242). It can also be used to decorate buttercream on the top of a cake.

7 Citrus zester

8 Cannelizing knife

9 Cook's knife

10 Plastic chopping board

11 Ice cream scoop

12 Spirit lamp

13 Rolling pin for nougatine

14 Set of oval fluted pastry cutters

15 Leaf mould for Sucre tiré

16 Painter's broad palette knife

17 Round-ended pastry brush for glazing

18 Beaumé scale or density saccharometer for measuring the density of the sugar in sorbet syrup or sorbet preparation. If the reading is too high, the sorbet will not set; if too low, the mixture will become icy and heavy. The correct reading is 16°Beaumé/1.1247 density. Sorbet syrup should be 30° Beaumé/1.2624 density.

19 Density measuring cup.

20 Mandoline

· PROFESSIONAL EQUIPMENT ·

1 Tray for large madeleines
Pastry cutters: **2** Holly leaf,
3 Pig, **4** Cat, **5** Duck, **6** Sitting
rabbit, **7** Heart, **8** Fish, **9**
Butterfly.
10 Assorted small pastry cutters
11 Assorted petits fours moulds
12 Supple, right-angled,
steel-bladed palette knife
13 Aluminium baking beans are
used for blind-baking tarts. They
are cleaner and heavier than the
dried beans; these are often too
light and let the pastry on the

bottom of the shell rise during
cooking, and they also tend to
burn, producing an unpleasant
smell.
14 Bakers' blades are the best
implement for slashing the bread
dough.
15 Skewers for fruits déguisés.
With a fruit déguisé on each end of
the skewer, dip each fruit into hard
crack sugar. Rest the skewer on a
rectangular mould set in a tray to
collect the drips, and allow the
sugar to cool. Large strawberries

and grapes are also delicious
dipped in sugar.
16 Rulers for fondant or Sucre
coulé (poured sugar)
17 Expanding sponge ring
18 Set of graduated pastry cutters
for vol-au-vents and Pithiviers
19 Large Croquembouche mould
20 Fondant saucepan
21 Small rectangular cake tin
22 Spiked plastic roller
23 Basketwork rolling pin. After
rolling marzipan to the desired
thickness and shape, use this

decorative rolling pin to roll over
the marzipan in one continuous
motion. Marked like this, the
marzipan should then be used
immediately to cover a whole cake
before it dries out.
24 Patisserie tray with raised edges
25 Plastic rolling pin achieves
smoothness on marzipan or
pastillage. It has a good weight.
26 Aluminium scoop for flour or
sugar
27 Rectangular straight-sided
cake tin

1 A chocolate warmer is an ideal piece of equipment for tempering and moulding when working with chocolate. It will melt and hold the chocolate at a constant temperature of between 30° and 35°C, depending on the couverture and the work to be done.
2 White chocolate
3 A chocolate thermometer, an essential tool which measures the chocolate temperature when using a bain-marie, rather than a chocolate warmer.
4 Scraper for making chocolate curls
5 Various sizes and shapes of chocolate holders and forks are employed for lifting the interior fillings out of the melted couverture and placing them on aluminium foil. The top of the chocolate can also be decorated with them before it sets.
6 Pouring ladle
7 Wooden spatula

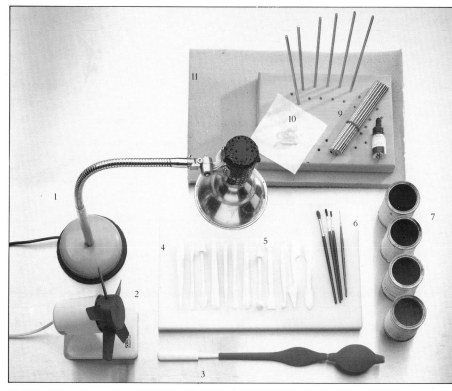

1 A sugar lamp can be either a reflective lamp mounted with an electric element (illustrated) or a warming lamp.
2 Electric fan
3 Sugar pump
4 Plastic sugar board
5 Sculpting tools for marzipan, chocolate or lard sculpture
6 Assorted paintbrushes for decorating
7 Powdered food colourings: blue, green, red and yellow
8 Acetic acid
9 Mandrin for weaving a basket in sugar. This one allows you to weave a basket in 2 different sizes. When the weaving is finished, remove the metal prongs and replace them with strips of Sucre tiré, placing the basket on a Sucre coulé base.
10 Cream of tartar
11 Foam pad

CHAPTER
· 2 ·

THE
BASIC RECIPES

These are the recipes which form the basis for all patisserie. From these are fashioned the tarts and flans, breads and croissants — all the delectable patisserie which *pâtissiers* love to display in their shop windows.

The various sponges are used as the base for charlottes, *bavaroises* and *délices* and are often brushed with a mixture of syrup and alcohol or fruit purée to enhance the flavour of the dessert. They are then topped or filled with mousses or custards made from meringue and cream mixtures and the resulting desserts are often served with a cream or fruit *coulis*.

PASTRY AND DOUGH

*T*he job of the *tourrier*, the person responsible for making dough, all pastes and dough products, is one of the most important in the art of patisserie. He is the point of departure for all the other pastry-cooks and his dough and pastes provide the foundation and guarantee of quality for all patisserie.

His job is fairly unrewarding compared to those who prepare the desserts and cakes; unlike him, they have the satisfaction of seeing the finished product. At the crack of dawn, and sometimes earlier, the *tourrier* is the first to arrive at the patisserie to prepare and shape his croissants and *brioches*. Then he cuts out his *mille-feuilles* and shapes his flans and tartlets.

Even uncooked dough gives off a delicious smell; the very texture and colour awaken the tastebuds. It is not unusual to see a *tourrier* who loves his work nibbling at his raw dough.

All dough keeps very well in the fridge for several days. It should be wrapped in clingfilm or polythene to prevent it from drying out and forming a crust. Dough can also be frozen successfully for several days.

PATE BRISEE
(Shortcrust)

· INGREDIENTS ·

250 g/9 oz flour
160 g/5½ oz butter, slightly softened
1 egg
Pinch of sugar
5 g/¾ tsp salt
1 tbsp milk

Makes about 475 g/1 lb 1 oz
Preparation time: 15 minutes

This light, crumbly, delicate shortcrust can be used as a substitute for puff pastry; it is particularly good for meat or fish *en croûte*. It can also be used as the crust for *pâté en croûte*, in place of the traditional pastry. It is always used to make classic flan and tartlet cases.

· PREPARATION ·

Place the flour on the work surface and make a well in the centre. Cut the butter into small pieces and place them in the well, together with the egg, sugar and salt. Rub in all these ingredients with the fingertips of your right hand, then, with your left hand, draw in the flour a little at a time. When all the ingredients are almost amalgamated, add the cold milk. Knead the dough with the palm of your hand 2 or 3 times

· EQUIPMENT ·

Marble or *wooden pastry board*
Greaseproof paper or *polythene*

until completely homogenous. Wrap in greaseproof paper or polythene and chill in the fridge for several hours before using.

· STORAGE ·

Wrapped in greaseproof paper or polythene, shortcrust will keep for several days in the fridge, or can be frozen for several weeks.

BRIOCHE

· INGREDIENTS ·

15 g/½ oz fresh yeast

70 ml/3 fl oz warm milk

15 g/2 tsp salt

500 g/1 lb 1 oz flour

6 eggs

350 g/12 oz butter, softened

30 g/1 oz sugar

1 egg yolk, lightly beaten with 1 tbsp milk

Serves 16

Preparation time: 20 minutes in an electric mixer, 35 minutes by hand

Rising and resting time: about 6 hours

Cooking time: 8 minutes for the small brioche (60 g/2 oz) 40-45 minutes for the large brioche

Weight: 1.2 kg/2 lb 10 oz

· EQUIPMENT ·

Electric mixer, or a large earthenware bowl

1 brioche mould for 16 people, 24 cm/9½ in diameter at the top, 11 cm/4½ in at the base or 1 18 cm/7 in copper saucepan or 20 small brioche moulds 8 cm/3¼ in diameter at the top, 4 cm/1½ in at the base

PICTURE PAGES 36-7

The essence of a perfect *brioche* is that it should have a delicious, rich, buttery flavour, yet leave no trace of butter on your fingers or aftertaste on the palate.

· PREPARATION ·

Place the yeast and warm milk in the mixer bowl and beat lightly with a wire whisk, then add the salt.

Add the flour and eggs and knead the dough with the dough hook or a spatula until it is smooth and elastic; this will take about 10 minutes in an electric mixer or 20 minutes by hand.

Beat the softened butter and sugar together, then, at low speed, add this mixture to the dough, a little at a time, making sure that it is completely amalgamated each time. Continue to mix for about 5 minutes in the mixer or 15 minutes by hand, until the dough is perfectly smooth. It should be glossy and shiny and fairly elastic.

Cover the bowl with a tea towel and leave in a warm place (about 24°C/75°F) for about 2 hours, until the dough has doubled in bulk.

Knocking back: Knock back the dough by flipping it over quickly with your fingertips not more than 2 or 3 times. Cover with a tea towel and place in the fridge for several hours (but not more than 24 hours).

Moulding and shaping: Place the dough on a lightly floured work surface and shape it into a large ball. If you are using a saucepan, line it with a sheet of buttered greaseproof paper twice the height of the pan. Place the dough in the saucepan.

If you are making the *brioche* in a mould, follow the step-by-step instructions opposite.

Lightly glaze the top of the *brioche* with eggwash, working from the outside inwards and taking care not to let any run into the cracks in the dough or onto the edges of the mould; this will prevent the dough from rising properly.

1

For a moulded brioche, cut off one-third of the dough to make the 'head'. Shape the larger piece into a ball and place in the mould. Press a hole in the centre with your fingertips.

2

With your hand at an angle, roll the 'head' into an elongated egg shape. Gently press the narrow end into the hole in the centre of the large ball with lightly floured fingertips.

1

2

3

After rising, glaze the top with eggwash, brushing from the outside inwards. Snip all around the edges of the large brioche with scissors dipped in cold water.

4

Bake immediately, then unmould on to a wire rack and leave to cool.

3

4

Rising: Leave to rise in a warm draught-free place until the dough has almost doubled in bulk (about 20 minutes for the small *brioches* and 1½ hours for a large one).

· TO COOK ·

Preheat the oven to 220°C/425°F/gas 8.

Lightly glaze the top of the *brioche* again, then snip all round the edges of the large *brioche* with scissors or a razor blade dipped in cold water. Do not snip the edges of the small *brioches*.

Bake immediately in the preheated oven for 40-45 minutes for the large *brioche*, 8 minutes for small ones.

Unmould immediately and place on a wire rack to cool.

Brioche looks very impressive if plaited or formed into a crown shape. For a real treat, cut it into slices, sprinkle with icing sugar and glaze under a very hot grill. Serve by itself for breakfast or, as a monstrous indulgence, warm with chocolate mousse.

· STORAGE ·

Brioche dough can be frozen, wrapped in polythene, after the knocking back stage. To bake, leave the dough to thaw gradually in the fridge for 4-5 hours, then proceed as above.

PATE A SAVARIN
(Savarin dough)

· INGREDIENTS ·

15 g/½ oz fresh yeast

200 ml/7 fl oz warm milk

15 g/2 tsp salt

500 g/1 lb 1 oz flour

6 eggs

150 g/5 oz butter, softened

15 g/½ oz sugar

Makes about 1.1 kg/2½ lb

Preparation time: 30 minutes in an electric mixer, 40 minutes by hand

· PREPARATION ·

Proceed exactly as for a *Brioche* (see page 32), but place only half the milk in the bowl with the yeast; reserve the other half and add it when the dough has become smooth and glossy and is fairly elastic. Add the milk, a little at a time, until the dough is more supple than for a *brioche*: it should not break when you stretch it between your fingers.

Cover the dough with a baking sheet or cloth and leave it to rise for 1 hour in a warm place (24°C/75°F). The dough should double in volume. Knock back the dough by flipping it once or twice with your hand. It is now ready to mould.

· NOTES ·

It is important not to let the dough rise too much, or the *savarins* will break when you soak them.

This dough will not keep, even in the fridge. It must be used within half an hour.

· EQUIPMENT ·

Electric mixer or a large earthenware bowl

1 saucepan

PATE A BLINIS
(Batter for blinis)

· INGREDIENTS ·

THE LEAVENING:

15 g/½ oz fresh yeast

250 ml/9 fl oz lukewarm milk

25 g/1 oz plain *or* wholemeal flour

THE BATTER:

125 g/4 oz plain *or* wholemeal flour

2 eggs, separated

Small pinch of salt

Makes about 500 g/1 lb 1 oz

Preparation time: 10 minutes, plus 3 hours resting

We use this batter mainly for *amuse-gueules*, like our *Blinis au caviar* (see page 193).

· PREPARATION ·

The leavening: In a bowl, whisk together the lukewarm milk and yeast, then add 25 g/1 oz flour. Cover the bowl with a plate and leave at room temperature (24°C/75°F) for 2 hours.

The batter: Using a spatula, stir in the flour and egg yolks. Cover with a plate and leave at room temperature for 1 hour.

The egg whites: Place in a bowl, beat well, then add a pinch of salt and beat until stiff. Fold them carefully into the batter. The batter is now ready to use.

· NOTES ·

Use the batter as soon as possible, and certainly within an hour, or it will ferment and the flavour will be spoilt.

· EQUIPMENT ·

2 bowls

PATE SUCREE
(Sweet short pastry)

· INGREDIENTS ·

250 g/9 oz flour
100 g/3½ oz butter
100 g/3½ oz icing sugar, sifted
Small pinch of salt
2 × 55-60 g/size 4 eggs, at room temperature

Makes about 520 g/1 lb 2 oz
Preparation time: 15 minutes

· EQUIPMENT ·

Marble or *wooden pastry board*
Greaseproof paper or *polythene*

This pastry is mainly used for tarts and tartlets, especially those which are baked blind and then filled with fresh fruit (eg, strawberry tart, which has a layer of *crème Chantilly* or *crème Chiboust* between the pastry base and the fruit). It is much easier to work than *pâte sablée*, which, being much finer, is difficult to roll out and shape.

Pâte sucrée is also less fragile when cooked, so it is perfect if you want a tart for a picnic or to transport.

· PREPARATION ·

Put the flour on the work surface and make a well in the centre. Cut the butter into small pieces, place them in the centre, then work with your fingertips until completely softened. Add the sugar and salt, mix well together, then add the eggs and mix. Gradually draw the flour into the mixture.

When everything is thoroughly mixed, work the dough 2 or 3 times with the palm of your hand until it is very smooth.

Roll the dough into a ball, flatten the top slightly, wrap in greaseproof paper or polythene and refrigerate for several hours.

· STORAGE ·

Wrapped in greaseproof paper or polythene, *pâte sucrée* will keep very well in the fridge for several days.

PATE A FONCER
(Lining or flan paste)

· INGREDIENTS ·

250 g/9 oz flour
125 g/4 oz butter, softened
1 × 60 g/size 3 egg
10 g/1½ tsp sugar
5 g/¾ tsp salt
40 ml/2 fl oz water

Makes about 480 g/1 lb
Preparation time: 15 minutes

· EQUIPMENT ·

Marble or *wooden pastry board*
Greaseproof paper or *polythene*

Traditionally, this dough is used as a base for flans and tartlets.

· PREPARATION ·

Proceed exactly as for *Pâte brisée*, adding the water when the dough is well mixed, but still a little crumbly and not completely homogenous. Knead the dough 2 or 3 times with the palm of your hand, until completely smooth. Wrap in greaseproof paper or polythene and chill in the fridge for several hours before using.

· STORAGE ·

Wrapped in greaseproof paper or polythene, it will keep for several days in the fridge, or can be frozen for several weeks.

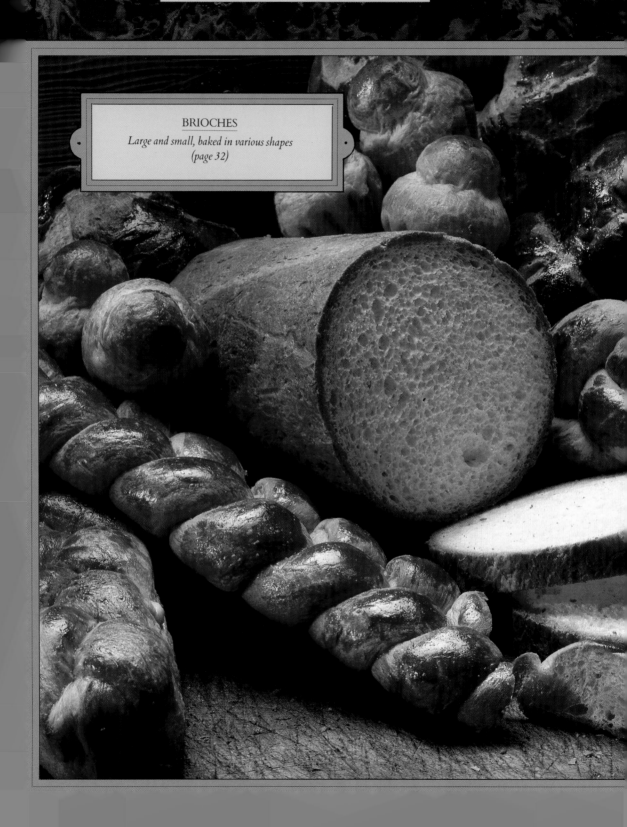

BRIOCHES

Large and small, baked in various shapes
(page 32)

CROISSANTS

· INGREDIENTS ·

40 g/1½ oz sugar
10 g/1½ tsp salt
300 ml/11 fl oz cold water
17 g/½ oz fresh yeast
25 g/1 oz milk powder
500 g/1 lb 2 oz strong flour
300 g/10 oz butter
1 egg yolk beaten with 1 tbsp milk, to glaze

Makes 16-18 croissants, 55-60 g/2 oz each
Preparation time: 1½ hours
Rising time: 2½ hours
Cooking time: 15 minutes

· PREPARATION ·

The dough: Prepare the dough 10-12 hours in advance.

Dissolve the sugar and salt in one-third of the cold water. In a separate bowl, beat the yeast into the remaining water with a small wire whisk, then beat in the milk powder.

Place the flour in the bowl of the electric mixer, then at low speed, using the dough hook, beat in first the sugar and salt mixture, then the yeast mixture. Stop beating as soon as the ingredients are well mixed and the dough comes away from the sides of the bowl. This should not take longer than 1½ minutes; do not overwork the dough.

Rising: Cover the dough with a tea towel and leave to rise in a warm place (about 24°C/75°F and not more than 30°C/86°F) for about 30 minutes. The dough should double in size.

Knocking back: Knock back the dough by quickly flipping it over with your fingers to release the carbon gases; do not overwork or the dough will be heavy. Cover with polythene and place in the fridge for 6-8 hours. (If the dough has risen again after an hour, knock it back again as described above.)

Rolling and shaping: Cut a cross in the top of the dough.

On a lightly floured surface, roll out the ball of dough in 4 places, making one-quarter turn each time, so that it looks like 4 large 'ears' around a small head.

Put the butter in the centre; it must be firm but not too hard, and about the same temperature as the dough. Fold the 4 'ears' over the butter, making sure that it is completely enclosed, so that the butter does not ooze out.

Lightly flour the work surface, then carefully roll the dough away from you into a rectangle about 40 × 70 cm/ 16 × 27 in. Brush off the excess flour from the surface of the dough. Fold the dough into 3. Wrap in polythene and refrigerate for at least 20 minutes. Repeat the process, rolling the dough in the opposite direction from before. Wrap and refrigerate as before. Repeat the process once more.

Roll out the dough to a 40 × 76 cm/16 × 30 in rectangle, flouring the work surface very lightly as you roll. Flap up the dough twice to aerate it and prevent shrinkage, taking care not to spoil the shape of the rectangle.

With a large knife, trim the edges, then cut the dough lengthways into 2 equal strips.

Lay one short edge of the triangular template along one long edge of the dough and mark out the outline with the back of the knife. Invert the triangle and mark out the outline as before. Continue in this way until you have marked out 16-18

· EQUIPMENT ·

Electric mixer
Wooden or *marble pastry board*
Isosceles triangular template, 14 × 18 cm/ 6 × 7 in

triangles, then cut them out with a sharp knife (marking out the shapes first will help to prevent mistakes).

Arrange the triangles on a baking sheet. Cover tightly with polythene and refrigerate for a few moments; if the dough becomes too warm, it may soften and crack.

Place the triangles, one at a time, on the work surface, with the long point nearest you. Stretch out the 2 shorter points, then, starting from the short edge, roll up the triangle towards you; use one hand to roll the dough and the other to pull down the long point. Make sure that the central pointed end is in the middle and underneath so that it does not rise up during cooking.

As soon as they are shaped, place the croissants on a baking sheet, turning in the corners in the direction of the pointed end to make a curved crescent shape. Since the sides of the oven are always the hottest, the last row of croissants must face backwards, or the points may dry out or burn.

Lightly brush the croissants with eggwash, working from the inside outwards, so that the layers of dough do not stick together, which would prevent the croissants from rising properly. Leave to rise in a very warm, humid and draught-free place (24°-30°C/75°-85°F) until they have doubled in size; this will take about 2 hours.

· TO COOK ·

Very lightly glaze the croissants again with eggwash. Preheat the oven to 230°C/450°F/gas 9. Bake the croissants in the preheated oven for 15 minutes, then transfer immediately to a wire rack, making sure that they are not touching.

· STORAGE ·

Croissants and *pains au chocolat* freeze very well for up to 2 weeks. Once they are baked and while they are still warm, wrap in plastic bags and freeze immediately. To serve, place, frozen, in an oven at 250°C/500°F/gas 10 for 5 minutes.

To freeze unbaked croissants, place on a baking sheet and freeze before they have risen at all. Leave to rise when you are ready to use. Do not freeze for longer than 8 days.

· FOR PETITS PAINS AU CHOCOLAT ·

While you are making the croissants, any large pieces of dough can be used to make *petits pains au chocolat*. Cut the dough into small rectangles, place one or two squares of plain chocolate on one side, then fold over the dough to make a small, flattish cylinder. Arrange on a baking sheet, glaze with eggwash, then proceed as for croissants, baking for 18 minutes. (Do not re-roll the trimmings; cook them just as they are to enjoy as nibbles.)

Continued overleaf

CROISSANTS

1

1
Shape the risen dough into a ball and cut a cross in the top.

2

2
On a lightly floured surface, roll out the dough in 4 places, making a quarter turn each time, leaving a raised platform in the centre, so that it resembles 4 ears surrounding a small head.

3

3
Place the chilled butter on the 'head'; butter and dough should be at the same temperature.

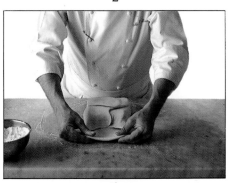

4

4
Fold the 4 'ears' over the butter, from front to back, to enclose it completely. Make sure the corners are tucked in so that the butter does not ooze out.

5

5
On a lightly floured surface, roll the dough into a rectangle about 70 × 40 cm/27 × 16 in. Brush off the excess flour from the surface of the dough.

6

6
Fold over the ends of the rectangle. Wrap in polythene and chill for at least 20 minutes.

7

7
Roll and fold the dough in the same way twice more, chilling it each time, until it has been rolled 3 times.

8

8
Roll out the dough into a 76 × 40 cm/30 × 16 in rectangle, lightly flouring the surface as you roll.

9

Flap up the dough twice to aerate it and to prevent it from shrinking. Take care not to spoil the shape of the rectangle.

10

Trim the edges of the dough, then draw the knife across the centre and cut the dough lengthways in half.

9

11

Lay a short edge of the triangular template along the long edge of the dough and cut. Invert the triangle and cut again. To avoid mistakes, mark out the shape with the back of a knife before cutting.

12

Lay the dough triangles in overlapping rows on a baking sheet. Cover tightly with clingfilm and leave to rest in the fridge.

 10

11

13

Place a dough triangle on the work surface with the long point nearest to you. Pull the long point downwards with one hand and roll up the triangle towards you with the other.

14

Fold the central point underneath the croissant. Place them on a baking sheet, turning the corners inwards to make a crescent.

 12

13

15

Arrange the croissants on the baking sheet in staggered rows. The back and front rows must face backwards, or the points may dry out and burn. Glaze with eggwash and leave to rise until doubled in size.

16

Lightly glaze the croissants again. Bake in a preheated oven, then transfer to a wire rack, spacing the croissants well apart.

14

15

16

FEUILLETAGE JEAN MILLET
(Jean Millet's puff pastry)

· INGREDIENTS ·

500 g/1 lb 1 oz flour, plus a little for 'turning'
200 ml/8 fl oz water
12 g/1¼ tsp salt
25 ml/1 fl oz white wine vinegar
50 g/2 oz butter, melted
400 g/14 oz butter, well chilled

Makes 1.2 kg/2½ lb

Preparation time: 1 hour 10 minutes, plus about 5 hours resting time

Many domestic cooks are terrified at the thought of making puff pastry, without just cause. It is certainly a lengthy process, but it is actually quite easy to make.

This recipe was created by our friend Jean Millet, the president of the Confédération de la Pâtisserie, Confiserie, Glacerie de France and MOF in patisserie.

· PREPARATION ·

The dough: Put 500 g/1 lb 1 oz flour on the work surface and make a well in the centre. Pour in the water, salt, vinegar and melted butter and work together with your fingertips. Using your left hand, gradually draw in the flour and mix well.

When all the ingredients are well mixed, work the dough with the palm of your hand until it is completely homogenous, but not too firm. Roll it into a ball and cut a cross in the top to break the elasticity. Wrap in polythene or greaseproof paper and chill in the fridge for 2 or 3 hours.

Incorporating the butter: Lightly flour the work surface. Roll out the ball of dough in four different places, so that it looks like 4 large 'ears' around a small, round head. Hit the chilled butter several times with a rolling pin, so that it is supple but still firm and very cold; place it on the 'head' so that it covers it with no overhang. Fold the 4 'ears' over the butter to cover it completely. Chill in the fridge for 30 minutes to bring the butter and dough to the same temperature.

Turning and folding: Lightly flour the work surface, then progressively roll the dough gently away from you into a rectangle about 70 × 40 cm/27 × 16 in. Fold over the ends to make 3 layers. This is the first turn.

Second turn: On the lightly floured surface, give the rectangle one-quarter turn and again progressively roll it gently away from you into a 70 × 40 cm/27 × 16 in rectangle. Fold the dough into 3. This is the second turn.

Wrap the dough in greaseproof paper or polythene and place in the fridge for 30 minutes to rest and firm up.

Make 2 more turns as above, then, after the fourth turn, wrap the dough and refrigerate again for 30 minutes to 1 hour.

Make 2 more turns, bringing the total to 6. The pastry is now ready to use.

· STORAGE ·

Well wrapped in greaseproof paper or polythene, the pastry will keep for up to 3 days in the fridge, or it can be frozen for several weeks. If you are going to store it, give it only 4 turns

· EQUIPMENT ·

Marble or wooden pastry board

Greaseproof paper or polythene

For the preparation of Puff pastry dough, refer to the Croissants recipe, steps 1–6 (see page 40).

and complete the 2 final turns on the day you use it. Replace the pastry in the fridge for 30 minutes after these 2 final turns.

· NOTES ·

Once you have cut the puff pastry into your desired shape (*bouchées, vol-au-vent, fleurons, feuilletés, palmiers,* etc) you must let it rest in a cold place for at least 30 minutes before baking, or the pastry will shrink and distort the shape.

Bake puff pastry in a hot oven, at 220°-240°C/425°-475°F/ gas 8-10.

FEUILLETAGE MINUTE
(Quick puff pastry)

· INGREDIENTS ·

1 kg/2 lb 2 oz flour, plus a pinch

1 kg/2 lb 2 oz butter, which should be firm but not too hard; (remove from the fridge 2 or 3 hours before using)

20 g/1 tbsp salt

500 ml/18 fl oz iced water (add ice cubes if necessary)

Makes about 2.5 kg/5½ lb
Preparation time: 20 minutes

· PREPARATION ·

Mixing the ingredients: Put the flour on the work surface and make a well in the centre.

Cut the butter into small cubes and put it into the well, together with the salt. Using your fingertips, work the ingredients together, gradually drawing in the flour with your left hand.

When the cubes of butter have become very small and half squashed and the mixture is becoming grainy, pour in the iced water and gradually incorporate it into the pastry. Do not knead it and stop working the pastry as soon as it becomes homogenous, but still contains some little flakes of butter.

Rolling: On a lightly floured surface, roll out the dough away from you into a 40 × 20 cm/16 × 8 in rectangle. Fold and proceed as for ordinary puff pastry (opposite), until you have made 2 turns. Wrap the pastry in greaseproof paper or polythene and chill in the fridge for 20 minutes.

Give the chilled pastry 2 more turns. It is now ready to use. Roll it to your desired shape, then place on a dampened baking sheet, as for classic puff pastry, and chill for 20 minutes before baking.

· STORAGE ·

This pastry is extremely quick and simple to prepare, but does not keep as long as classic puff pastry — only 2 days in the fridge or 3 days in the freezer. Wrap it in greaseproof paper or polythene to store.

· NOTES ·

Quick puff pastry will rise about 30 per cent less than the classic type.

· EQUIPMENT ·

Marble or wooden pastry board

Greaseproof paper or polythene

LEFT *Wholemeal and white bread rolls and loaves (pages 48–51)*
ABOVE *Pain de mie (page 51)*

PATE A CHOUX
(Choux paste)

· INGREDIENTS ·

125 ml/4½ fl oz water

125 ml/4½ fl oz milk

100 g/3½ oz butter, cut into small pieces

3 g/½ tsp fine salt

5 g/¾ tsp sugar

150 g/5 oz flour

4 × 60 g/size 3 eggs

Makes 22-25 choux buns or éclairs

Preparation time: 20 minutes

Cooking time: 10-20 minutes, depending on the size and shape of the buns

---

Choux paste is enormously versatile, which makes it a marvellous, indispensable component of all types of cooking and patisserie.

· PREPARATION ·

Preheat the oven to 220°C/425°F/gas 7.

Cooking the paste: Put the water, milk, diced butter, salt and sugar in a saucepan, set over high heat and boil for 1 minute, stirring with a spatula. Take the pan off the heat and, stirring all the time, quickly add the sifted flour.

The next stage — the 'drying out' — is vitally important if you want to make good choux paste. When the mixture is very smooth, replace the pan over the heat and stir with the spatula for 1 minute.

The paste will begin to poach and some of the water will evaporate. Be very careful not to let the paste dry out too much, or it will crack during cooking and your buns or éclairs will not be perfectly smooth. Tip the paste into a bowl.

Adding the eggs: Immediately beat in the eggs, one at a time, using a spatula. Stir well until the paste is very smooth; it is now ready to use. If you do not want to use it immediately, spread one-third of a beaten egg over the surface to prevent a skin or crust from forming, which may easily happen after a few hours.

Piping the paste: Choose an appropriate plain nozzle to pipe out your chosen shape — small or large choux buns, éclairs, swans, *Paris-Brest* or whatever.

Pipe out the paste on baking parchment or a greased baking sheet. If you like, glaze the shapes and mark them lightly with the back of a fork, dipping it into the glaze each time.

· EQUIPMENT ·

1 saucepan

1 fine sieve

1 bowl

1 baking sheet

Baking parchment (optional)

Piping bag with a plain nozzle

Bake in the preheated oven, then open the oven door slightly (about 1-2 cm/¾ in) after 4 or 5 minutes and leave it ajar. Cooking time will vary from 10-20 minutes, depending on the size of the buns.

· STORAGE ·

Stored in an airtight container, choux paste will keep for 3 days in the fridge, or for up to 1 week in the freezer.

PATE SABLEE
(Shortbread dough)

· INGREDIENTS ·

RECIPE 1:

250 g/9 oz flour

200 g/7 oz butter

100 g/3½ oz icing sugar, sifted

Pinch of salt

2 egg yolks

1 drop vanilla *or* lemon essence (optional)

RECIPE 2:

30 g/1 oz ground almonds

250 g/9 oz flour

140 g/5 oz butter

100 g/3½ oz icing sugar, sifted

1 egg

Pinch of salt

1 drop vanilla *or* lemon essence (optional)

Makes about 680 g/1½ lb (recipe 1)
600 g/1¼ lb (recipe 2)
Preparation time: 15 minutes

· PREPARATION RECIPE 1 ·

Sift the flour onto the work surface and make a well in the centre. Dice the butter and place it in the well, then work it with your fingertips until very soft. Sift the icing sugar onto the butter, add the salt and work into the butter. Add the egg yolks and mix well. Gradually draw in the flour and mix until completely amalgamated. Add the vanilla or lemon essence, if you are using it, and rub it into the dough 2 or 3 times with the palm of your hand.

· RECIPE 2 ·

Sift together the ground almonds and flour onto the work surface and make a well in the centre. Proceed as for recipe 1.

Roll the dough into a ball and flatten it out lightly. Wrap in greaseproof paper or polythene and chill in the fridge for several hours.

· STORAGE ·

Wrapped in greaseproof paper or polythene, both doughs will keep very well in the fridge for several days.

· NOTES ·

Flour is always the last ingredient to be added to *pâte sablée*, so that the dough remains crumbly and 'short'. Once you have added the flour, do not overwork the dough, or it will become too elastic. Recipe 1 is very delicate; if you are using the dough to line a flan tin or to make *sablés*, you must work very fast, without overhandling the dough, as it softens extremely quickly. Rolled and cut into different shapes, it is perfect for *petits fours secs*.

Recipe 2 is easier to make, roll out and handle, but because it contains less butter, it is less rich and delicate.

· EQUIPMENT ·

Wooden or *marble pastry board*

1 fine sieve

Greaseproof paper or *polythene*

BREAD

*T*here is one simple reason why French bread has often been imitated but never equalled — nothing goes into it but flour, water, salt and yeast. French flour is different from British flour.

Bread-making is a subject in its own right, which we cannot cover fully here, but we feel we must at least mention the different types of flour used in Britain. The recipes in this chapter are for breads which we bake every day in our restaurants; they are all simple to make at home. We find them extremely satisfying and we know you will too!

We list below a few important definitions:

Extraction ratio is the percentage of flour obtained from a given quantity of wheat.

The ratio of particles or mineral content determines the flour type. The whiter the flour, the fewer impurities it contains, and the lower its bran ratio will be. The main flour types are graded according to their percentage of bran per 100 grammes of dry matter.

The main flour types, characteristics and uses:

Wholemeal or whole wheat flour: Extraction rate 100%, protein 12%, carbohydrate 64.3%, dietary fibre 11.2%. This flour contains the whole wheat grain; nothing is added or taken away during processing.

Uses: Breads, rolls and special bread rolls.

Wheatmeal or brown flours: Extraction rate 85-90%, protein 11.8%, carbohydrate 68.5%, dietary fibre 7.8%.

Uses: Breads, bread rolls and in certain cakes and specialities.

'Strong' white flour – bakers' grade: Extraction rate 70-75%, protein 11.3% minimum (some strong flours have 12-13% protein), carbohydrate 71.5%, dietary fibre 3.15%.

Uses: The most popular type used for all white bread and all other yeast-raised products, puff paste and choux paste.

'Soft' or cake flour, made with an addition of weaker British and other European wheats: Extraction rate 55-75%, protein 8-8.6%, carbohydrate and dietary fibre percentage vary depending on the brands of flour as can the percentage of the extraction rate and protein.

Uses: For all cake making, sponges, biscuits, soft pastes eg. short, sweet etc.

The moisture content is normally 15% for all flours. The 'strength' of the flour refers to the quality as well as the quantity of gluten-forming protein present in the respective flours.

Other flours (rye, rice, soya and cassava): These are often used as improving agents or for flouring around the bread before baking. Rye flour, with a little wheat flour added, is used to make rye bread (*pain de seigle*).

LE PAIN
—— *(Bread rolls)* ——

· PREPARATION ·

The bread can be made either by hand or in an electric mixer.

By hand: Put the flour, sugar and salt into a bowl or basin and make a well in the centre.

In a separate bowl, combine the yeast and water and pour

· INGREDIENTS ·

450 g/1 lb strong flour
30 g/1 oz sugar
15 g/2 tsp salt
15 g/½ oz fresh yeast
250 ml/9 fl oz water at 16°C/60°F

Makes 15–20 rolls
Preparation time: 35 minutes
Rising time: 2½ hours
Cooking time: about 12 minutes

· EQUIPMENT ·

1 large mixing bowl or an electric mixer
1 baking sheet
Clingfilm

PICTURE PAGES 44-5

into the well. Mix with your hand until the ingredients are thoroughly blended, drawing the flour gradually into the liquid. Do not overwork.

Using an electric mixer: Combine the water and yeast in the bowl and beat lightly with a whisk. Add the flour, salt and sugar and beat, using the dough hook, at the lowest speed until completely homogenous.

Rising: When the dough has reached this stage, leave it in a warm place (about 24°C/75°F), covered with a damp cloth or a baking tray. Leave to rise or 'prove' for about 2 hours; the dough should have doubled in bulk. Knock back the dough by quickly flipping it over with your fingers not more than 2 or 3 times.

Shaping: Place the dough on a marble or wooden surface. Using a sharp knife, divide it into even pieces of the size you require. Shape the dough into rounds or pull into long rolls and place them on a baking sheet.

Make small incisions, 5 mm/¼ in deep in the top of the long rolls, using a razor blade set in a cork, so as not to cut yourself, or use bakers' blades or scissors. Make a cross in the top of the round rolls.

Cover the rolls with clingfilm to prevent them from drying out and forming a crust and to protect them from draughts. Leave in a warm place (about 24°C/75°F) for about 30 minutes to rise again or 'prove'. If you want the rolls to be a deep amber colour, glaze them with beaten egg just before baking.

· TO COOK ·

Preheat the oven to 240°C/475°F/gas 10.

Place a few small tins full of water in the bottom of the oven; these will give off enough steam to bake the bread perfectly. Bake the rolls in the preheated oven for about 12 minutes. If you like a shiny finish, as soon as you take them out of the oven, brush each roll with a very slightly moistened brush.

· STORAGE ·

To freeze the rolls, wrap them in clingfilm and put them in the freezer as soon as they have cooled; they will taste freshly baked if you use them within a few days. It is essential to warm them in a moderate oven (190°C/375°F/gas 6) for about 5 minutes before serving. By keeping a stock of rolls in the freezer, you can enjoy fresh bread every day without having to bake it daily.

PAIN COMPLET
(Wholemeal rolls)

· INGREDIENTS ·

THE LEAVENING:

15 g/½ oz fresh yeast

500 ml/18 fl oz water warmed to 16°C/61°F

250 g/9 oz strong flour

250 g/9 oz wholemeal flour

THE DOUGH:

600 g/1¼ lb strong flour

600 g/1¼ lb rye flour

35 g/1 oz salt

500 ml/18 fl oz water warmed to 16°C/61°F

Makes 60 rolls, 40-45 g/ about 1½ oz each

Preparation time: 35 minutes

Rising time: 5½ hours

Cooking time: about 20 minutes

· PREPARATION ·

The leavening: In a large bowl, dissolve the yeast in the water and add the 2 flours. Mix gently without overworking the mixture and set aside in a warm place (about 24°C/75°F) for at least 1 hour, but not more than 2 hours. The leavening should double in volume.

The dough: This can be made either by hand or in an electric mixer.

By hand: Mix the 2 flours in a bowl and make a well in the centre. Mix together the salt and water and pour it into the well, then add the leavening. Mix with your hand until completely homogenous, gradually drawing the flour into the middle. Do not overwork the dough, which should be firm and have some body.

Using an electric mixer: Put the leavening and the salt dissolved in water in the bowl, then add the flours. Beat at the lowest speed until completely homogenous; do not overwork the dough, which should be firm and have some body.

Rising: Cover the bowl with a damp cloth or baking sheet and leave to rise in a warm place (about 24°C/75°F) for about 3 hours. The dough should double in bulk.

Shaping: Knock back the dough by flipping it over quickly with your fingers not more than 2 or 3 times.

Place the dough on a marble or wooden surface and shape it into evenly sized balls, about 40-45 g/1½ oz each.

Place on a baking sheet. Make small crosses, 5 mm/¼ in deep, in the top of the rolls, using a razor blade set in a cork so as not to cut yourself, or use bakers' blades or scissors.

Cover the rolls with clingfilm to prevent them from drying out and forming a crust and to protect them from draughts. Leave in a warm place (about 24°C/75°F) for about 1½ hours to rise again or 'prove'.

· TO COOK ·

Preheat the oven to 240°C/475°F/gas 10. Place a few tins full of water in the bottom of the oven; these will give off enough steam to bake the rolls perfectly.

Bake the rolls in the preheated oven for about 20 minutes.

· STORAGE ·

To freeze the rolls, wrap them in clingfilm and put in the freezer as soon as they have cooled; they will taste freshly baked if you use them within a few days. It is essential to warm

· EQUIPMENT ·

2 large mixing bowls or an electric mixer

2 baking sheets

Clingfilm

PICTURE PAGES 44-5

them in a moderate oven (190°C/375°F/gas 6) for about 5 minutes before serving.

· NOTES ·

A little flour sprinkled lightly over the rolls before baking will give a nice rustic effect. The same dough can be used to make 1 or 2 'country' loaves which, since they are larger, will take longer to bake. Allow about 45 minutes cooking time for 1 kg/2 lb 2 oz dough.

PAIN DE MIE
(White bread)

· INGREDIENTS ·

750 g/1 lb 10 oz strong flour

30 g/1 oz sugar

20 g/1 tbsp salt

250 ml/9 fl oz lukewarm milk, warmed to about 30°C/86°F

125 ml/5 fl oz water, warmed to 16°C/61°F

3 eggs

60 g/2 oz butter, melted and cooled

30 g/1 oz fresh yeast

50 g/2 oz butter, for greasing

Makes 1 loaf

Preparation time: 20 minutes

Rising time: 2 hours 45 minutes

Cooking time: 40-45 minutes

· PREPARATION ·

The bread can be made either by hand or in an electric mixer.
By hand: Put the flour, salt and sugar in a bowl and make a well in the centre. In a separate bowl, combine the yeast, warmed milk and water and pour into the well. Mix with your hand until all the ingredients are well blended, drawing the flour gradually into the liquid. Do not overwork.

Add the eggs, one by one, then the cooled melted butter. Work the dough with your hand until it comes away cleanly from the sides of the bowl; it should be smooth, compact and elastic.

Using an electric mixer: Combine the water, milk and yeast in a bowl and beat lightly with a whisk. Add the flour, salt and sugar and, using the dough hook, mix at the lowest speed until almost homogenous. Add the eggs, one at a time, then the cooled melted butter. Continue to beat at low speed until the dough comes away from the sides of the bowl; it will now be smooth, compact and elastic.

Rising: When the dough has reached this stage, leave it in a warm place (about 24°C/75°F), covered with a damp cloth or a baking tray. Leave to rise or 'prove' for about 2 hours, then knock back the dough by flipping it over quickly with your fingers not more than 2 or 3 times.

Shaping: Place the dough on a marble or wooden surface and either plait it or divide it into 4 equal parts and form each into a round ball. Generously butter the loaf tin and put in the plait or the 4 balls, one beside the other.

Cover with clingfilm to prevent the dough from drying out and forming a crust and to protect it from draughts.

Leave in a warm place for about 45 minutes, until the dough has risen to within about 2 cm/1 in from the top of the tin.

Preheat the oven to 220°C/425°F/gas 8.

· EQUIPMENT ·

1 large mixing bowl or an electric mixer

1 black metal rectangular loaf tin, about 41 × 11 cm/ 16 × 4½ in, 10 cm/4 in deep, with a sliding lid

Clingfilm

PICTURE PAGES 44-5

· TO BAKE ·

If you want a loaf with 4 nicely rounded bumps on top and a light, airy texture, do not cover the tin with the lid. If, however, you prefer a rectangular loaf with a closer texture, slide the lid onto the tin. Do not cover the plait, or you will spoil the shape. Bake in the preheated oven for 40-45 minutes.

As soon as you take the bread from the oven, remove the lid if you have used it, taking care not to scald yourself. Unmould the loaf onto a wire rack and leave until completely cold.

· STORAGE ·

To freeze the loaf, wrap it in clingfilm when it is barely cold and freeze at once; it will taste as good as if it were freshly baked when you come to use it. Heat the bread at 190°C/375°F/gas 6 for 10 minutes before serving.

PAIN AUX NOIX
(Walnut bread)

· INGREDIENTS ·

500 g/1 lb 1oz wholemeal flour

5 g/¾ tsp salt

50 g/2 oz brown sugar

25 g/1 oz fresh yeast

4 tbsp water, heated to 16°C/61°F

60 g/2 oz butter

250 ml/9 fl oz milk, warmed to 30°C/86°F

35 g/1 oz shelled walnuts

50 g/2 oz butter, for greasing

Makes 1 loaf

Preparation time: 25 minutes

Rising time: 1 hour 45 minutes

Cooking time: 35 minutes

· PREPARATION ·

The walnut bread can be made by hand or in an electric mixer.
By hand: Put the flour, salt and brown sugar in a bowl and make a well in the centre. In a separate bowl, mix the yeast and water.

Cook the butter in the saucepan until it is nutty brown, then pass through a conical strainer onto the milk and stir in the yeast mixture.

Pour the mixture into the well, a little at a time, and gently draw the flour into the middle. Mix with your hand until thoroughly blended; do not overwork.
Using an electric mixer: Combine the water, milk, browned butter and yeast in the bowl and stir with a whisk. Add the flour, salt and sugar and, using the dough hook, beat at the lowest speed until thoroughly blended.
Rising: Coarsely chop the walnuts and mix them into the dough. Cover the bowl with a damp cloth or baking tray and leave to rise or 'prove' in a warm place (at about 24°C/75°F) for about 1 hour.

When the dough has proved, knock it back by flipping it over quickly with your fingers not more than 2 or 3 times.
Shaping: Generously grease the loaf tin or terrine, roll the dough into a long sausage shape and place in the mould. Cover with clingfilm to prevent the dough from drying out and a skin from forming, and to protect it from draughts. Leave in a warm place to rise for about 45 minutes.

Preheat the oven to 220°C/425°F/gas 8.

· EQUIPMENT ·

1 large mixing bowl or an electric mixer

1 cast iron terrine mould or a black metal rectangular loaf tin about 32 × 8 cm/ 13 × 3 in, 8cm/3 in deep

1 small saucepan

1 conical strainer

Clingfilm

· TO BAKE ·

Bake the loaf in the preheated oven for 35 minutes, then turn out onto a wire rack.

· STORAGE ·

This bread is at its best 2 days after baking. To freeze, wrap it in clingfilm when barely cold and freeze at once. Don't reheat it before eating; simply take it out of the freezer 3 or 4 hours in advance. It is delicious with cheese.

SPONGE AND DESSERT BASES

*T*hese bases are made to be filled, masked or decorated but they can be served on their own, although of course they would be less attractive this way. Children enjoy them served plain for tea and they are excellent for those gourmets who prefer their cake without cream. They will keep for several days in a cool, dry place, wrapped in clingfilm. As most can be frozen successfully, you will always have a home-made cake to offer; fill the base with whipped cream and some strawberries or seasonal fresh fruit or simply surround it with a light *crème anglaise*.

BISCUITS
—— *(Sponge biscuits for bases, Swiss rolls and fingers)* ——

· INGREDIENTS ·

RECIPE 1:
4 whole eggs
3 egg yolks
85 g/3 oz sugar
35 g/1 oz flour
40 g/1½ oz potato flour

Makes 1 Swiss roll
60 × 40 cm/24 × 16 in

Sponge biscuits are used as a base for numerous desserts, from the simplest to the most elaborate. They can be served simply filled with jam or marmalade, with *crème Chantilly* (see page 66) or chocolate *ganache* (see page 197), but they are also used for almost all charlottes and some decorative *pièces montées*.

· PREPARATION ·

The eggs: Separate them and put the yolks in one bowl and the whites in another.
The yolks: Beat them with two-thirds of the sugar until they form a ribbon.
The whites: Beat in the mixer until well risen, then add the

· EQUIPMENT ·

Electric mixer
1 sifter
1 flan ring or sponge tin,
22 cm/8½ in diameter,
4 cm/1½ in deep
1 baking sheet, 60 × 40 cm/
24 × 16 in
Greaseproof paper or baking
parchment
Piping bag, with plain
nozzles of various sizes

RECIPE 2:

6 eggs
190 g/6½ oz sugar
180 g/6 oz flour
30 g/1 oz icing sugar, for sponge fingers

Makes 1 round sponge, about 22 cm/8½ in diameter, 4 cm/1½ in deep

Preparation time: 20 minutes

Cooking time: varies according to the thickness of the biscuits

remaining sugar and beat at high speed for 1 minute until firm.

Mixing the yolks and whites: Using a flat slotted spoon, fold about one-third of the whites into the yolks until the mixture is perfectly blended. Tip in the remaining whites all at once and fold them very gently into the mixture. Before it is thoroughly blended, still mixing continuously, scatter in the sifted flour and the potato flour, if you are using Recipe 1. As soon as the mixture is homogenous, stop mixing, or it will become heavy.

Shaping and baking the sponge: The baking time will depend on the shape, thickness and size of the biscuits.

To pipe a rolled biscuit (using Recipe 1): Use a piping bag fitted with a plain nozzle, which can be any size from 5 mm/¼ in to 1.5 cm/½ in, depending on the desired shape. Alternatively, use a ridged nozzle or a palette knife. Pipe or spread the mixture onto a sheet of baking parchment or lightly buttered and floured greaseproof paper.

Slide the paper onto a baking sheet and bake in a hot oven at 220°C/425°F/gas 8 for about 6 minutes, if you are using the 5 mm/¼ in nozzle. Allow longer for a larger nozzle.

The cooked sponge should be about 5 mm/¼ in thick. Invert it onto a tea towel and immediately and carefully peel off the paper. Fill and roll the sponge, as for the *Igloo Douillet* (page 108) or assemble it in layers, alternating the sponge with flavoured cream.

To pipe sponge fingers (using Recipe 2): With a piping bag fitted with a 1.5 cm/½ in nozzle, pipe out 'fingers' about 10 cm/4 in long onto baking parchment or lightly buttered and floured greaseproof paper. Lightly dust them twice with icing sugar, at 5 minute intervals. Bake in a hot oven at 220°C/425°F/gas 8 for 8-10 minutes. Before the sponge fingers have cooled completely, lift them off the paper with a palette knife and place on a wire rack.

To make bases for desserts and centrepieces (using Recipe 2): Pour the mixture into a lightly buttered and floured tin or flan ring and bake in a moderate oven at 190°C/375°F/gas 5 for 15-25 minutes, depending on the diameter of the mould, and therefore on the thickness of the sponge.

As soon as the sponge is cooked, invert it onto a wire rack. Rotate it one-quarter turn every 15 minutes until it has cooled completely to prevent it from sticking to the rack.

· STORAGE ·

Sponge fingers should be eaten on the day they are made; after 2 or 3 days, they dry out and crumble and lose all their delectable moistness.

BISCUIT JOCONDE

in our *Palmerosa* (see page 129).

· INGREDIENTS ·

375 g/13 oz *tant pour tant* (equal quantities of icing sugar and ground almonds, sifted together)

5 whole eggs

5 egg whites

25 g/1 oz sugar

40 g/1½ oz butter, melted and cooled

50 g/2 oz flour

30 g/1 oz butter, plus a pinch of flour, for greasing

Makes about 900 g/2 lb (enough for one sponge, 60 × 40 cm/24 × 16 in)

Preparation time: 15 minutes

Cooking time: 2-3 minutes

· EQUIPMENT ·

Electric mixer

1 bowl

1 baking sheet, 60 × 40 cm/ 24 × 16 in

Greaseproof paper or baking parchment

Wire rack

Biscuit joconde is a very fine, delicate sponge which is used to make all kinds of desserts based on mousses and *bavaroises*, and in our *Palmerosa* (see page 129).

· PREPARATION ·

Preheat the oven to 250°C/500°F/gas 10.

The whole eggs: Put the eggs and *tant pour tant* in the bowl of the mixer and beat at high speed for about 10 minutes, until the mixture forms a ribbon. Pour into a bowl and set aside.

The egg whites: Beat until well risen, then add the sugar and beat faster for 1 minute.

The mixture: Using a flat slotted spoon or spatula, fold the cooled butter, then the flour into the whole egg mixture.

Mix in one-third of the egg whites until thoroughly blended, then fold in the rest, taking care not to overmix.

· TO COOK ·

Using a palette knife, spread the sponge mixture over a sheet of baking parchment or lightly buttered and floured greaseproof paper, to a thickness of about 3 or 4 mm/⅛ in. Bake immediately in the very hot oven for 2-3 minutes. To test whether the sponge is cooked, touch it with your fingertips. It should not stick to your fingers, but be just firm, yet moist and on no account dry.

Slide the cooked sponge, still on the paper, onto a wire rack. Remove the paper only just before using the sponge.

· STORAGE ·

This sponge freezes well; freeze it, still on the paper, either flat or rolled up like a Swiss roll, which takes up less space.

B I S C U I T   A   L ' O R A N G E
(Orange sponge biscuit)

· INGREDIENTS ·

4 × 55 g/size 4 eggs
1 × 70 g/size 2 egg
85 g/3 oz finely ground almonds
Zest of ½ orange, finely chopped
25 g/1 oz candied orange peel, very finely chopped
130 g/4½ oz sugar
85 g/3 oz flour, plus a pinch for the mould
1 tsp melted butter

Serves 8
Preparation time: 15 minutes
Cooking time: 25 minutes

This Orange sponge biscuit is used in the recipes for *Rozenn au parfum d'orange mentholé* (see page 112) and *Alméria* (see page 136). It can also be used to make plain biscuits which are delicious served with tea.

· PREPARATION ·

Preheat the oven to 200°C/400°F/gas 7.

The eggs: Separate the eggs and put the yolks in one bowl and the whites in another.

Add the ground almonds, chopped orange zest, candied peel and three-quarters of the sugar to the yolks and beat together until the mixture forms a ribbon.

Beat the whites until soft peaks form, then add the remaining sugar and beat until very stiff.

Mixing the yolks and whites: Using a flat, slotted spoon, fold one-third of the egg whites into the yolk mixture and blend thoroughly. Gently fold in the remaining whites. Just before the whites are completely incorporated, sift in the flour, stirring continuously. Stop stirring as soon as the flour is completely amalgamated.

· TO COOK ·

Brush the inside of the tin or ring with melted butter and coat lightly with flour. Place the ring on a baking sheet lined with baking parchment or buttered and floured greaseproof paper.

Gently pour in the sponge mixture and level the surface with a pastry scraper or palette knife.

Bake the sponge in the preheated oven for 25 minutes. As soon as it is cooked, turn it onto a wire rack and remove the outer ring.

· STORAGE ·

This sponge can be baked 24 hours in advance and keeps very well for up to 48 hours.

· EQUIPMENT ·

Electric mixer
1 loose-bottomed flan or cake tin or Genoise sponge ring 22 cm/9 in diameter, 3.5 cm/1¼ in deep
1 baking sheet
Greaseproof paper or baking parchment

M E R I N G U E   S U I S S E
(Swiss meringue)

· INGREDIENTS ·

4 egg whites (125 ml/ 4 fl oz or 40 g/4½ oz)
300 g/10 oz sugar

This meringue has a firmer, more solid texture than French meringue and is perfect for making decorations or for dessert bases. It is not, however, as delicate and melting as French meringue.

Preparation time: 20 minutes

Cooking time: 1 hour 45 minutes

· PREPARATION ·

Combine the egg whites and sugar in the mixing bowl. Stand the bottom of the bowl in a bain-marie set over direct heat. Beat the mixture continuously until it reaches a temperature of about 40°C/104°F.

Remove the bowl from the bain-marie and continue to beat until the mixture is completely cold.

· PIPING AND COOKING ·

Preheat the oven to 120°C/250°F/gas 1.

Spoon the mixture onto baking parchment or lightly buttered and floured greaseproof paper, using 2 soup spoons, or use a piping bag fitted with different nozzles to pipe it into various shapes and sizes.

Lower the oven temperature to 100°C/200°F/gas ½ and cook the meringues for 1 hour 45 minutes. They are ready when both the top and bottom are dry.

· EQUIPMENT ·

Electric mixer or a copper bowl and whisk

Bain-marie

Greaseproof paper or baking parchment

Piping bag and plain or decorative nozzles, depending on the desired effect

MERINGUE FRANCAISE
(French meringue)

· INGREDIENTS ·

4 egg whites (125 ml/ 4 fl oz or 140 g/4½ oz)

125 g/4 oz sugar

125 g/4 oz icing sugar, sifted

Preparation time: 15 minutes

Cooking time: 1 hour 45 minutes

· PREPARATION ·

Whisk the egg whites until soft peaks form. Beat in the sugar, a little at a time, and continue to beat for 10 minutes. The mixture should be firm and very smooth and shiny.

Gradually sift in the icing sugar, folding it gently into the mixture with a slotted spoon. Do not overwork the mixture. Use the meringue immediately.

· PIPING AND COOKING ·

Preheat the oven to 120°C/250°F/gas 1.

Pipe or spoon the mixture onto baking parchment or lightly buttered and floured greaseproof paper, using 2 soup spoons or a piping bag fitted with the appropriate nozzle.

Lower the oven temperature to 100°C/200°F/gas ½ and cook the meringues for 1 hour 45 minutes. They are ready when both the top and bottom are dry.

· STORAGE ·

Meringues will keep very well for up to 2 weeks in an airtight tin or tightly sealed container. Keep in a dry place.

· NOTES ·

You should always keep a few prepared meringue shells or cases ready for impromptu meals. You can then rustle up a marvellous dessert by combining the meringue with some

· EQUIPMENT ·

Electric mixer or a copper bowl and whisk

Greaseproof paper or baking parchment

Piping bag and plain or patterned nozzles, depending on the desired effect

whole fruits or a fruit mousse, some whipped cream, ice cream or a sorbet.

If you prefer a pale golden meringue, cook it at 150°C/300°F/gas 3, but reduce the cooking time by about 30 minutes.

MERINGUE ITALIENNE
(Italian meringue)

· INGREDIENTS ·

80 ml/3 fl oz water

360 g/12 oz sugar

30 g/1 oz glucose (optional)

6 egg whites

Preparation time: 7 minutes

Cooking time: 15–20 minutes

· PREPARATION ·

Cooking the sugar: Put the water in the copper pan, then add the sugar and glucose, if using. Place over moderate heat and stir the mixture with a skimmer until it boils. Skim the surface and wash down the sugar crystals which form inside the pan with a brush dipped in cold water. Now increase the heat so that the syrup cooks rapidly. Insert the sugar thermometer to check the temperature.

The egg whites: When the sugar reaches 110°C/230°F, beat the egg whites in an electric mixer until stiff. Keep an eye on the sugar and take the pan off the heat when it reaches 121°C/248°F.

Mixing the sugar with the egg whites: When the egg whites are well risen and firm, set the mixer to the lowest speed and gently pour on the cooked sugar in a thin stream, taking care not to let it run onto the whisks. Continue to beat at low speed until the mixture is almost completely cold; this will take about 15 minutes. The meringue is now ready to use.

· STORAGE ·

Meringue italienne can be kept in the fridge for several days, stored in an airtight container.

· NOTES ·

The glucose prevents crystals from forming in the egg whites or at the edge of the bowl when the sugar is added.

The quantity of sugar used in this recipe may vary, depending on how the meringue will be used. If you want a light meringue, 50 g/2 oz sugar per egg white will be enough; if, however, you need a very firm, stiff mixture, you will need 70 g/2½ oz sugar for each white.

The quantities given here are the smallest possible needed to achieve a really good result.

You can make an excellent buttercream using *Meringue italienne* (see page 66).

· EQUIPMENT ·

1 copper sugar pan

Sugar thermometer

Electric mixer

FOND DE PROGRES AUX AMANDES OU NOISETTES

(Almond or hazelnut meringues 'Japonais')

· INGREDIENTS ·

6 egg whites

250 g/9 oz *tant pour tant*, (equal quantities of icing sugar and ground almonds *or* hazelnuts, sifted together)

30 g/1 oz sugar

30 g/1 oz butter, for greasing

15 g/½ oz flour, plus a pinch for dusting

30 g/1 oz flaked almonds *or* hazelnuts

Makes 3 × 20 cm/8 in diameter bases, or 24 × 5 cm/2 in diameter bases

Preparation time: 20 minutes

Cooking time: 1 hour for the large bases, 40 minutes for the small ones

The almonds and hazelnuts make this a more sophisticated mixture than plain meringue.

· PREPARATION ·

Preheat the oven to 150°C/300°F/gas 3.

The egg whites: Beat until soft peaks form, then add the sugar and beat until firm.

Scatter in the *tant pour tant* and 15 g/½ oz flour and fold into the whites with a flat slotted spoon, stopping as soon as they are well mixed. Do not overwork.

Piping the mixture: Line the baking sheet with baking parchment or buttered and floured greaseproof paper. Draw your desired shape on the paper, or press the cutters into the flour to mark out the shape. Leave plenty of space between the circles.

Starting from the centre of the circles, pipe out the mixture in a spiral, using the 1 cm/½ in nozzle for the larger circles and the 5 mm/¼ in nozzle for the individual bases. Sprinkle with flaked almonds or hazelnuts and bake at once in the preheated oven.

· TO COOK ·

Cook the large bases for 1 hour and the small ones for 40 minutes, or until they are completely dry, like meringues, and a pale, creamy colour.

· TO SERVE ·

Cover one of the bases with *crème mousseline* (see page 63), chocolate or coffee *Chantilly* (see page 66), or *crème pralinée* (see page 63) and top with another circle, then make a third layer in the same way. Serve this simple, luscious dessert as soon as possible. To make it even more special, garnish with fruits in season and a *coulis* made from the same fruits and poured around the edge in a ribbon.

· STORAGE ·

These bases will keep very well for 8-10 days, stored in an airtight container in a dry place. Keep some handy in case of unexpected guests.

· EQUIPMENT ·

Electric mixer, or a bowl and whisk

1 baking sheet

Flan ring or pastry cutters to mark out the shapes

Piping bag with a plain nozzle, 5mm /¼ in for the small bases, 1 cm/½ in for the large bases

Greaseproof paper or baking parchment

and replace under the grill until lightly caramelized. Leave to cool completely.

When the nuts have cooled, chop them with a knife, or crush coarsely with a rolling pin.

Fold them into the *crème pralinée* at the very last moment so that they remain crunchy.

· STORAGE ·

You can keep it in the fridge for up to 2 days in an airtight container, but it will have lost some of its exquisite lightness when you come to use it. Remove the cream from the fridge an hour before using, then beat lightly to restore its smoothness, but not, alas, its original volume.

SAUCE CARAMEL
(Caramel sauce)

· INGREDIENTS ·

80 ml/3 fl oz water

100 g/3½ oz sugar

500 ml/18 fl oz double cream

2 egg yolks, lightly beaten (optional)

Makes about 700 ml/1¼ pints

Preparation time: 5 minutes, plus chilling

· EQUIPMENT ·

1 large saucepan

1 bowl

Conical strainer

PICTURE PAGES 68-9

Caramel sauce makes a quite delicious accompaniment to numerous desserts. It should be served very cold. It can also be churned in an ice cream maker to make a caramel ice cream.

· PREPARATION ·

Cooking the sugar: Pour the water into a large saucepan and add the sugar. Set over low heat until the sugar has completely melted and is beginning to boil. Wash down the inside of the pan with a pastry brush dipped in cold water to prevent any crystals from forming. Cook the sugar until it turns a lovely deep amber and the surface begins to smoke slightly. Take the pan off the heat immediately and beat in the cream, stirring constantly with a whisk.

Cooking the sauce: Set the pan back over a high heat and stir with the whisk. Let the mixture bubble for 2 or 3 minutes, then remove from the heat.

Still stirring, pour a little of the sauce onto the egg yolks, then return this mixture to the pan but do not cook it. Pass the sauce through a conical strainer into a bowl and keep in a cool place. Stir the sauce from time to time to prevent a skin from forming.

· STORAGE ·

The sauce will keep in the fridge for up to 48 hours stored in an airtight container.

· NOTES ·

The egg yolks are not essential, but they do make the sauce smoother, less liquid and more refined.

CREME D'AMANDE
(Almond cream)

· INGREDIENTS ·

· INGREDIENTS ·

250 g/9 oz butter

500 g/1 lb 2 oz *tant pour tant* (equal quantities of icing sugar and ground almonds sifted together)

50 g/2 oz flour

5 eggs

50 ml/2 fl oz rum (optional)

Makes 1 kg 150 g/2½ lb
Preparation time: 20 minutes

This cream forms the basis of several desserts, particularly *Pithiviers* and various tarts. It can be made moister and more velvety by stirring in 20-30 per cent of *crème pâtissière* just before using.

· PREPARATION ·

Work the butter with the beater or spatula until very soft. Still beating, work in the *tant pour tant* and the flour, then the eggs one by one, beating between each addition. The mixture should be light and homogenous. Stir in the rum.

· STORAGE ·

The cream will keep very well for 4 or 5 days; keep it in the fridge in an airtight container or a bowl covered with clingfilm. Take it out of the fridge 30 minutes before using.

· EQUIPMENT ·

Electric mixer or food processor with a paddle beater or flat whisk or mixing bowl and spatula

PICTURE PAGES 68-9

CREME AU CHOCOLAT
(Chocolate cream)

· INGREDIENTS ·

200 ml/7 fl oz double cream

150 g/5 oz sugar

120 g/4 oz cocoa powder, sifted *or* unsweetened bitter chocolate, chopped

300 g/10 oz butter, at room temperature

Makes about 750 g/1 lb 10 oz
Preparation time: 15 minutes, plus cooling

This chocolate cream is very rich and velvety, without being sickly. It is used mostly in biscuit- and sponge-based desserts and all sorts of chocolate confections, from the simplest to the most elaborate.

· PREPARATION ·

Cooking the cream: Put the cream and sugar in a saucepan, place over high heat and bring to the boil, stirring continuously. Boil for 3 minutes, then take the pan off the heat and whisk in the cocoa or chopped chocolate and half the butter, a little at a time. Pour the mixture into a bowl and leave in a cool place until completely cold. Whisk from time to time to prevent a skin from forming.

Combining the butter with the cream: In the electric mixer, or a bowl, beat the remaining butter for 3 minutes, until very light. Still beating, incorporate the cold chocolate cream, 1 spoonful at a time and beat for about 5 minutes, until the mixture is homogenous and very light in texture, almost like a mousse. The cream is now ready to use.

· STORAGE ·

The cream keeps very well for up to 3 days in the fridge, stored in an airtight container.

· EQUIPMENT ·

1 saucepan
Electric mixer or a bowl and whisk

PICTURE PAGES 68-9

CRÈME AU BEURRE
(Buttercream)

· INGREDIENTS ·
250 ml/9 fl oz water
700 g/1 lb 8 oz sugar
50 g/2 oz glucose
(optional)
9 egg whites
1 kg/2 lb 2 oz butter, at
room temperature

Makes about 2.3 kg/5 lb
Preparation time: 20
minutes, plus cooling·
Cooking time: 15–20
minutes

Buttercream made with *meringue italienne* is a simple, easy-to-make cream, which can be used in many recipes, including all sorts of biscuit- and sponge-based desserts. Its great advantage is that it is neither too rich nor too sickly and so is easily digestible.

· PREPARATION ·

The meringue italienne: Make the meringue with all the ingredients except the butter, following the recipe given on page 58.
Adding the butter: When the meringue is almost cold, set the mixer on low speed and beat in the butter, a little at a time. Beat for about 5 minutes, until the mixture is very smooth and homogenous. The buttercream is now ready to use.

· STORAGE ·

It will keep well in the fridge for up to a week stored in an airtight container. Before using the buttercream, leave at room temperature for 1 hour, then mix well until smooth.

· EQUIPMENT ·
1 copper sugar pan
Sugar thermometer
Electric mixer

PICTURE PAGES 68-9

CRÈME CHANTILLY
(Plain, chocolate and coffee)

· INGREDIENTS ·
FOR ALL THE CREAMS:
500 ml/18 fl oz whipping
cream, well chilled
50 g/2 oz icing sugar
or 50 ml/2 fl oz Sorbet
syrup (see page 168)
Vanilla powder or
extract, to taste
(optional)
FOR THE
CHOCOLATE CREAM:
150 g/5 oz plain
chocolate or 2 tbsp
cocoa powder, sifted
FOR THE COFFEE CREAM:
1 tbsp hot milk
2 tbsp instant coffee or
1 tbsp coffee extract

Crème Chantilly is used to lighten and enrich numerous creams — the *crème pâtissière* in an *Alméria* (see page 136) for example. It can also be served just as it is and will complement many desserts, fruits and ice creams.

· PREPARATION ·

Plain crème Chantilly: Combine the well-chilled cream with the sugar or sorbet syrup and vanilla in a chilled mixer bowl and beat at medium speed for 1 or 2 minutes. Increase the speed and beat for 3 or 4 minutes, until the cream begins to thicken. Do not overbeat, or the cream may turn into butter. It should be a little firmer than the ribbon stage.
Chocolate Chantilly: Melt the plain chocolate in a double boiler; the temperature should not exceed 35°C/95°F. Remove from the heat and whisk in one-third of the plain *crème Chantilly*. Fold gently and delicately into the remaining *crème Chantilly;* do not overwork the mixture.

If you are using cocoa instead of the plain chocolate, add it when you beat the cream.

· EQUIPMENT ·
Electric mixer or a bowl and
whisk, chilled

PICTURE PAGES 68-9

Makes about 600 g/1 lb 4 oz
Preparation time: 8 minutes

Coffee Chantilly: Dissolve the coffee in the hot milk and leave to cool. Add it when you beat the cream. Alternatively, add a tablespoon of coffee extract when you whip the cream.

· STORAGE ·

It is best to use the *Chantilly* as soon as you have made it, but it can be kept in the fridge in an airtight container for up to 24 hours.

· NOTES ·

If you haven't any whipping cream, but only double cream, add some very cold milk to the cream before whipping. You will need 15 per cent of the volume of the cream (which will be about 75 ml/3 fl oz). Proceed as for whipping cream.

SAUCE CHOCOLAT
(Chocolate sauce)

· INGREDIENTS ·
200 g/7 oz bitter
chocolate *or* plain
couverture
150 ml/5 fl oz milk
2 tbsp double cream
30 g/1 oz sugar
30 g/1 oz butter

Makes about 460 g/1 lb
Preparation time: 10
minutes

Chocolate sauce is used as the base for innumerable desserts, ice creams etc. Served hot, it is delicious with profiteroles, vanilla ice cream and *Soufflé tiède aux poires* (see page 151). Served cold, it adds the finishing touch to a *vacherin* or a slice of toasted *brioche*.

· PREPARATION ·

The chocolate: Melt it in the double saucepan or a bain-marie.
To cook the sauce: Put the milk, cream and sugar in a saucepan and set over high heat. Stir gently with a whisk until the mixture boils. Pour it onto the melted chocolate, stirring constantly. Tip the whole mixture into the saucepan and let it bubble for 15 seconds.

Take the pan off the heat and beat in the butter, a little at a time, until the sauce is completely homogenous. Pass through a conical strainer.

· STORAGE ·

The sauce keeps very well in the fridge for up to 3 days; store it in a bowl covered with clingfilm, or in an airtight container.

· EQUIPMENT ·
Double saucepan or
bain-marie
1 *saucepan*
Conical strainer

PICTURE PAGES 68-9

6

2

3

4

5

1 Coulis de fruits rouges (page 71); 2 Crème
d'amande (page 65); 3 Crème pralinée (page 63);
4 Crème ganache (page 197); 5 Sauce caramel
(page 64); 6 Gelée de pommes (page 70);
7 Crème au chocolat (page 65); 8 Crème
Chiboust (page 62); 9 Crème pâtissière (page 61);
10 Crème au beurre (page 66); 11 Crème
mousseline (page 63); 12 Sauce chocolat (page
67); 14 Crème anglaise (page 70); 15 Crème
Chantilly (page 66).

1

7

8

9

10

11

12

14

15

CREME ANGLAISE
(Custard cream)

· INGREDIENTS ·
12 egg yolks
250 g/9 oz sugar
1 lt/1¾ pt milk
1 vanilla pod, split

Makes about 1.55 lt/2½ pints
Preparation time: 15 minutes
Cooking time: 8 minutes
approximately

Crème anglaise is used as a base for numerous desserts, sweets and ice creams. It is delicious served like a *coulis* or sauce with cakes or red fruits; serve it well chilled.

· PREPARATION ·

Put the egg yolks in a bowl with one-third of the sugar (about 85 g/3 oz). Beat with a whisk until the mixture forms a ribbon.

· TO COOK ·

Combine the milk, split vanilla pod and the remaining sugar in a saucepan and bring to the boil. Pour the boiling milk onto the egg mixture, whisking continuously.

Pour the mixture back into the pan, set over low heat and cook, stirring continuously with a spatula, until the custard is thick enough to coat it. On no account let the custard boil.

Pass the custard through a conical strainer and keep in a cool place until completely cold. Stir from time to time to prevent a skin from forming.

· STORAGE ·

The custard keeps very well in the fridge for 2 or 3 days. Pass it through a conical strainer again before serving.

· NOTES ·

If you prefer a much less rich and creamy sauce, you can reduce the number of egg yolks, but do not use fewer than 8 yolks for each litre (1¾ pints) of milk.

The vanilla pod can be replaced by 3 tablespoons of instant coffee or 100 g/3½ oz melted plain chocolate.

· EQUIPMENT ·
1 bowl
1 saucepan
1 conical strainer

PICTURE PAGES 68-9

GELEE DE POMMES
(Apple jelly)

· INGREDIENTS ·
500 ml/18 fl oz water
250 g/9 oz sugar
500 g/1 lb 2 oz eating
apples (preferably Cox's)
6 leaves of gelatine

This delicately flavoured apple jelly is translucent, which makes it ideal for 'neutral' glazes where no colour is required. It is perfect for all kinds of mousse-based desserts, like our *Délice aux fruits de la passion* (see page 132) and adds a beautiful sheen. It can also be used to coat peeled fruits to prevent them from discolouring or drying out, and it makes a good glaze for fruit tarts.

· EQUIPMENT ·
1 saucepan with a lid
Conical strainer or a jelly
bag
1 bowl

PICTURE PAGES 68-9

Makes 500 ml/18 fl oz

Preparation time: 20 minutes

Cooking time: about 15 minutes

· PREPARATION ·

The syrup: Pour the water into the pan and add the sugar. Heat until the sugar has dissolved completely and is beginning to boil, stirring with a whisk from time to time. Skim the surface if necessary.

The gelatine: Soak the leaves in cold water for 20 minutes, then drain.

The apples: Wash or wipe them, but do not peel. Coarsely chop the whole apples, including the core, and drop them into the boiling sugar syrup. Cover the saucepan and simmer for about 7 minutes. Take the pan off the heat and push the apples to one side so that you can drop in the drained gelatine and dissolve it. When it has dissolved, pass the mixture carefully through a conical strainer or jelly bag set over a bowl.

Use the jelly as a glaze for various desserts when it is cold, but before it begins to set.

· STORAGE ·

The jelly will keep in an airtight container for up to 4 days. Reheat it, then leave to cool again before using.

COULIS DE FRUITS
(Fruit coulis)

· INGREDIENTS ·
800 g/1 lb 12 oz fresh fruit (eg, strawberries, raspberries, wild strawberries, redcurrants, pineapple, apricots, peaches, kiwi fruit)
Juice of 1 lemon
250 ml/9 fl oz Sorbet syrup (see page 168)

Makes about 800 g–1 kg/ 1lb 12 oz–2 lb 2 oz, depending on the density of the fruit
Preparation time: 15 minutes

Fruit *coulis* go wonderfully well with all kinds of desserts, from mousses to tarts, gâteaux and ice creams. Almost any fruit is suitable for this *coulis*, depending on the desired flavour, but do not mix different fruits.

· PREPARATION ·

Wash, drain, hull, peel or core the fruit as appropriate. Place in the blender or food processor with the lemon juice and syrup and process until smooth. Pass through the strainer and keep in the fridge until you are ready to use the *coulis*.

· STORAGE ·

Fruit *coulis* freeze very well; beat well as soon as they have thawed. You can perfectly well use bottled or tinned fruits in syrup instead of fresh fruit. Use only 125 ml/4 fl oz sorbet syrup and top it up with the same amount of water.

· NOTES ·

Allow at least 100 ml/4 fl oz of *coulis* per person.

Two tablespoons of fruit *coulis* in a glass of champagne makes the most delectable cocktail.

· EQUIPMENT ·
Blender or food processor
1 conical strainer

PICTURE PAGES 68-9

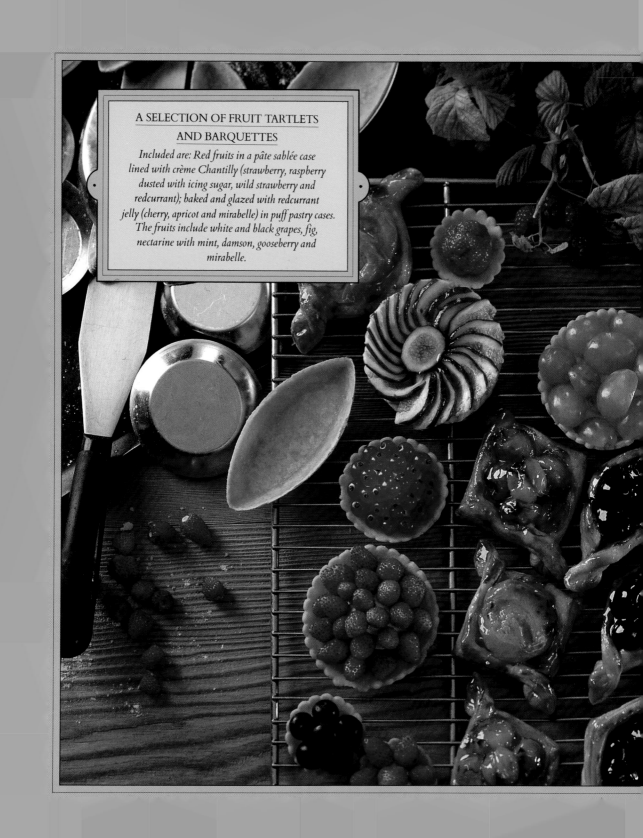

A SELECTION OF FRUIT TARTLETS
AND BARQUETTES

*Included are: Red fruits in a pâte sablée case
lined with crème Chantilly (strawberry, raspberry
dusted with icing sugar, wild strawberry and
redcurrant); baked and glazed with redcurrant
jelly (cherry, apricot and mirabelle) in puff pastry cases.
The fruits include white and black grapes, fig,
nectarine with mint, damson, gooseberry and
mirabelle.*

CHAPTER
· 3 ·

DESSERTS

*R*ichly-hued, light and delicate, a dessert should add the final flourish, like the royal seal on a regal missive. The preparation, therefore, demands a great deal of attention and a modicum of patience.

In France, the country of gastronomy, desserts have always played a very important part in family gatherings and social occasions as well as in religious festivals: yule logs at Christmas, *galettes des rois* at Epiphany, chocolate eggs and animals at Easter. Baptisms, first communions and weddings are occasions for towering *croquembouches* or *pièces Bretonnes*, while Mother's Day inspires cakes decorated with love and affection.

We French associate a large, fine cake with joyful occasions and shared friendship.

Nowadays, it is quite usual for guests to present their hostess with a beautiful pastry instead of a bunch of flowers. Even though fellow guests may not be hungry by this stage of the meal, if the dessert is simple, original and unusual, no one will resist a taste.

· USING FRUIT IN DESSERTS ·

Fruit is the best-loved and most sought after of all natural ingredients. Whether frozen, bottled or canned, but best of all fresh, it is the pre-eminent natural product — fruit is the king!

Its sugar, juice and pure flavour makes it the most delicate of all ingredients in any dessert; there is nothing to beat it. There is no limit to its uses — virtually all fruits will grace any cake or gateau — hence the ever-growing demand from the customer for every type of fruit.

Even out of season, thanks to refrigerated air and road transport, we can always obtain fresh red fruits from Europe, particularly Italy, Spain and France. Thus from late May right through until October, city dwellers always find raspberries and strawberries, with their sweet flavour and delicate scent.

Depending on the fruits you use and the effect you want to create, you can produce all manner of desserts — light, refreshing, sweet or sharp-tasting; no one will be able to resist the shimmering, appetizing colours of a fruit dessert.

· WHAT TO DRINK WITH DESSERTS ·

If you want to devote your tastebuds entirely to the delights of the dessert, you should drink only iced water; however, if you are feeling festive and want to marry a wine with your pudding, remember that the wine you choose should vary according to the type of pudding and the season of the year; depending on whether the dessert is very sweet or not and on the basic ingredients — fruits, chocolate, sponge biscuit or mousse. The appropriate wine could be Sauternes and Barsac, Beaumes de Venise, Monbazillac, Banyuls or medium dry white or pink champagne. A medium sweet cider can make a delicious accompaniment.

T A R T S

*W*arm or cold (but never chilled), tarts can be served on almost any occasion; after lunch, for tea, at a buffet or even after dinner. We have never been able to resist that most seductive lure of a little tartlet, filled with wild strawberries, accompanied of course by those scintillating little bubbles which one finds in a glass of pink champagne!

Make different pastry cases to suit the occasion; the type will vary according to the kind of fruit you use, the preferences of your guests and the time of day when you are going to serve the tart. After dinner, for example, it is best to use a fine, light, delicate pastry, such as puff pastry or trimmings, *pâte sucrée* or *sablée;* for tea, a *brioche* dough, shortcrust or flan pastry would be more suitable.

Adorned with exotic fruits like mangoes and lychees, their iridescent colours and fragrances make them truly alluring. Even decorated with such humble fruits as apples and pears, they are still delicious, though more simple and rustic.

As children, we adored helping our mother to roll out the pastry and to decorate the

Continued on page 78

· T A R T S ·

TOP LEFT *Tarte chaude aux deux fruits (page 88)*
BOTTOM LEFT *Tarte aux mirabelles (page 79)*
ABOVE *Tarte al'coloche (page 93)*

1

Spread all the butter thickly and evenly over the base of the pan or heatproof dish.

2

Pour over the sugar.

3

Arrange the peeled, cored and halved apples, rounded side down.

4

Loosely roll the pastry on to the rolling pin, then unroll it over the apples.

5

Tuck in the pastry at the edge of the pan and trim off the excess with a knife.

6

When the tart is cooked, carefully invert it on to a round dish, using a cloth to protect your arms and hands, as it will be very hot.

TARTE DES DEMOISELLES TATIN
(Tart Tatin)

PICTURE PAGES 82-3

· INGREDIENTS ·

6 medium dessert
apples, preferably Cox's

Juice of ½ lemon

120 g/4 oz butter

200 g/7 oz sugar

250 g/9 oz Puff pastry or
trimmings
(see pages 42-3)

Pinch of flour

Serves 4

Preparation time: 20
minutes plus 20 minutes
resting time

Cooking time: 40 minutes

· EQUIPMENT ·

Deep frying pan or round
heatproof dish, 26 cm/10 in
diameter, 7 cm/2¼ in deep

Wooden or marble pastry
board

This easy-to-make winter pudding makes a pleasant change from a classic apple tart. Don't eat it too greedily, or you may burn your tongue on the delicious golden caramel coating the apples!

· PREPARATION ·

Preheat the oven to 220°C/425°F/gas 8.

The apples: Peel, core and halve them. Sprinkle with lemon juice and place in the fridge.

Assembling the tart: Evenly grease the base of the frying pan or dish with butter. Cover the bottom of the pan with the sugar, then arrange the apples, rounded side down, on the bottom of the pan.

On a lightly floured surface, roll out the puff pastry into a circle about 3 mm/⅛ in thick. Lay the pastry over the apples, allowing an overlap of about 2 cm/¾ in all round. Trim off the excess with a sharp knife.

Leave to rest in a cool place for at least 20 minutes.

· TO COOK ·

Set the pan or dish over fierce direct heat for 15–20 minutes, until the butter and sugar are bubbling and have become a deep amber colour. With a small palette knife, lift a little of the pastry away from the edges to ensure even cooking.

Cook in the preheated oven for 20 minutes, until the pastry is risen and golden.

· TO SERVE ·

As soon as the tart is cooked, invert it quickly onto a round serving dish, taking care not to burn yourself. The pastry will now be on the bottom of the plate, with the apples on top. If any have slipped, push them back into place with a small knife. Serve the tart piping hot.

· NOTES ·

For an original variation on a classical idea, make small individual tarts Tatin using mangoes instead of apples and halving the quantity of butter. Serve with a *coulis* made from equal quantities of mango and passion fruit.

1 and 4 *Tarte princesse aux pruneaux* (page 84); 2 and 3 *Tarte des Demoiselles Tatin* (page 81); 5 and 6 *Tarte marguerite* (page 85); 7 and 11 *Tarte aux perles de groseilles* (page 92); 9 and 10 *Tarte aux fruits de saison: Reine Claude and quetsches* (page 91); 8 and 12 *Tarte aux noisettes* (page 78)

TARTE PRINCESSE AUX PRUNEAUX
(Prune tart 'Princess')

· INGREDIENTS ·

520 g/1 lb 2 oz *Pâte à foncer* (see page 35) or puff pastry trimmings

2 pinches of flour

30 g/1 oz butter, for greasing

Eggwash, made with 1 egg yolk and 1 tbsp milk

900 ml/1½ pt double cream

7 eggs

250 g/9 oz sugar

Finely grated zest of 1 orange

50 soft prunes, stoned and steeped in 150 ml/5 fl oz Armagnac for about 15 minutes

1 quantity *Crème Chiboust* (see page 62), with 1 leaf of gelatine added

50 g/2 oz sugar, to glaze

Makes 2 tarts, each serving 8

Preparation time: 30 minutes, plus 20 minutes chilling

Cooking time: 45 minutes

· PREPARATION ·

Preheat the oven to 220°C/425°F/gas 8.

The pastry cases: On a lightly floured surface, roll out half the pastry into a circle about 2 mm/1/16 in thick.

Grease a flan ring, place on a baking sheet and line the ring with the pastry. Pinch up the edges so they come about 4 mm/1/4 in above the ring. You will have about 30 g/1 oz pastry left over. Repeat the operation for the second pastry case.

Leave to rest in the fridge for at least 20 minutes.

Baking blind: Prick the pastry bases with a fork or the point of a knife. Line them with greaseproof paper or foil and fill with baking beans. Bake in the preheated oven for 15 minutes.

Remove the paper and beans, then brush the insides of the cases with eggwash and bake for a further 5 minutes, or until the glaze is lightly coloured. Set aside, in the rings, at room temperature. Reduce the oven to 200°C/400°F/gas 7.

The cream filling: Combine the double cream, eggs, sugar and grated orange zest in a bowl and mix lightly together.

Baking the tarts: Spread the prunes over the bottom of the pastry cases and pour over the cream mixture. Bake at 200°C/400°F/gas 7 for 25 minutes, until the cream has set.

Take the tarts out of the oven and, with a small knife, trim the crimped edges so that they are almost level with the cream filling. Slide a knife blade between the flan ring and the tart and lift off the ring, rotating it a quarter turn as you do so. Place on a wire rack and leave at room temperature.

Decorating and glazing: Heat the glazing iron over a gas flame, or switch it on if it is electric; alternatively, preheat the grill. Pipe the *crème Chiboust* onto the tarts in stars or rosettes so that the surface of the tarts is raised by about 2 cm/3/4 in.

Sprinkle the surface with sugar and touch the top of each star or rosette for barely 1 second with the hot iron, to make a thin layer of caramel. Alternatively, place the tarts under the hot grill until the sugar caramelizes.

· TO SERVE ·

Serve the tarts whole not more than 2 or 3 hours after filling them, and let your guests help themselves.

· NOTES ·

Since it is difficult to reduce the quantities for the *Tarte princesse* without spoiling the proportions, it is better to make

· EQUIPMENT ·

Wooden or marble pastry board

2 flan rings, 22 cm/8½ in diameter, 3 cm/1¼ in deep

1 baking sheet

Greaseproof paper or foil

Baking beans

Glazing iron or grill

1 bowl

Piping bag fitted with a 1 cm/½ in plain or patterned nozzle

PICTURE PAGES 82-3

2 at one time. The second tart can be frozen, unglazed, for up to 3 days. To serve, place in the fridge to thaw gradually for 3 or 4 hours, then leave it at room temperature for another 2 or 3 hours, and finally glaze it just before serving.

Dried apricots make a delicious substitute for the prunes.

Gelatine is added to the *crème Chiboust* to help it hold its shape when it is caramelized.

TARTE MARGUERITE TUTTI FRUTTI
(Marguerite tart)

· INGREDIENTS ·

150 g/5 oz Puff pastry
(see pages 42-3) *or*
trimmings, *or Pâte
brisée* (see page 31)

Pinch of flour

Eggwash, made with
1 egg yolk and
1 tbsp milk

250 ml/9 fl oz *Pâte à
choux* (see page 46;
½ recipe quantity)

350 g/12 oz *Crème
Chantilly*
(see page 66)

150 g/5 oz each of
various fruits:
eg: gooseberries,
blackberries, wild
strawberries, cherries,
golden raspberries,
bilberries, loganberries,
washed and hulled as
necessary

Sprig of fresh mint, to
garnish

Serves 7

Preparation time: 30
minutes

Cooking time: 35 minutes

This unusual tart with its rainbow colours presents an interesting contrast between the soft choux pastry and the crisp puff pastry. You can substitute other seasonal fruits.

· PREPARATION ·

Preheat the oven to 200°C/400°F/gas 7.

The pastry base: On a lightly floured surface, roll out the pastry as thinly as possible (about 1 mm/¹⁄₁₆ in) into a circle. Roll the circle on to a rolling pin, then unroll it on to a dampened baking sheet. Place the flan ring or template on the pastry and, with a sharp knife, cut around the outside edges following the contours of the mould. You will have about 50 g/2 oz pastry left over.

Lift off the flan ring and prick the pastry with a fork. Glaze the outside edges with eggwash, then brush lines of eggwash from the points where the rounded edges meet towards the centre to mark out 7 sections (see diagram).

The choux paste: Pipe out the choux paste following the lines of eggwash, then glaze the choux paste with eggwash. Leave to rest at room temperature for 5 minutes.

· TO COOK ·

Bake the prepared base in the preheated oven for about 35 minutes. Using a palette knife, slide the base on to a wire rack and keep at room temperature.

· TO SERVE ·

The base can be baked several hours in advance, but should only be filled at the last moment. Spread 50 g/2 oz *crème Chantilly* inside each choux pastry triangle and fill each with a different kind of fruit. Garnish the centre of the tart with a sprig of mint and serve at once.

· EQUIPMENT ·

Wooden or marble pastry
board

1 baking sheet

1 daisy-shaped flan ring, or
a template with 7 rounded
edges, 26 cm/10 in
diameter (see diagram)

Piping bag with a plain
1 cm/½ in nozzle

PICTURE PAGES 82-3

ABOVE *Tarte à l'orange (page 89)*
RIGHT *Tarte au citron (page 90)*

TARTE CHAUDE AUX DEUX FRUITS
(Hot two-fruit tart with sabayon sauce)

200 g/7 oz Puff pastry trimmings (see pages 42-3) or Pâte brisée (see page 31)

Pinch of flour

5 crisp dessert apples, (about 500 g/1 lb 1 oz) preferably Cox's

75 g/2½ oz butter

60 g/2 oz sugar

75 ml/3 fl oz Calvados

80 g/3 oz bilberries in syrup, drained or 50 fresh bilberries poached in syrup

4 egg yolks

Serves 4

Preparation time: 35 minutes

Cooking time: 15 minutes

This delicate tart is very quick and easy to make.

· PREPARATION ·

Preheat the oven to 240°C/475°F/gas 10.

The pastry: On a lightly floured surface, roll out the pastry into a circle about 24 cm/9 in diameter and 2 mm/¹/₁₆ in thick. Place on a baking sheet brushed with cold water and prick the surface with a fork or a sharp knife. Leave to rest in the fridge.

The apples: Peel, halve and core them, then cut each half into ten even slices. Place in the sauté pan with the butter and sauté over high heat for 1 minute. Add the sugar, then flambé with 15 ml/1 tbsp of the Calvados. Drain the apples and keep the cooking juices and the apples separately in a cool place.

Assembling the tart: Arrange the cold apples in an attractive rosette pattern on the pastry base.

Cooking: Bake the tart in the preheated oven for 12 minutes.

Drain the bilberries thoroughly and arrange them in little heaps on top of the apples. Sprinkle 30 g/1 oz of the sugar over the top and return the tart to the oven for a further 3 minutes.

The sabayon sauce: In a shallow pan, combine the egg yolks, the remaining Calvados, 1 tablespoon water and the cooking juice from the apples. Set the pan over gentle, indirect heat or in a bain-marie and beat the mixture continuously with a whisk until you have a very smooth lukewarm froth (about 50°C/120°F).

· TO SERVE ·

Serve the tart on a round china plate, or, better still, on the baking sheet. Serve the sauce separately in a sauceboat, or poured around the tart in a ribbon, if you are using individual plates.

· NOTES ·

Never make the *sabayon* sauce more than 10 minutes before serving, or it will lose its frothiness. If you prefer, you can make individual tartlets instead of 1 large tart. Try adding a thin layer of 2 tablespoons *crème pâtissière* between the pastry base and the apples for a real treat.

Wooden or *marble pastry board*

Baking sheet

1 sauté pan

1 shallow pan

1 strainer

PICTURE PAGE 76

TARTE A L'ORANGE
(Orange tart)

· EQUIPMENT ·

Wooden or marble pastry board

1 flan ring, 22 cm/8½ in diameter, 2 cm/¾ in deep, or a loose-bottomed flan tin

1 baking sheet

Pastry crimper

Cannelizing knife

1 small saucepan

1 large, deep dish

Wire rack

PICTURE PAGE 86

· INGREDIENTS ·

380 g/13 oz *Pâte sucrée* (see page 35)

Pinch of flour

Butter, for greasing

250 g/9 oz *Crème d'amande* (see page 65)

150 g/5 oz (about 5 tbsp) *Crème pâtissière* (see page 61)

2 large oranges, total weight about 600 g/ 1 lb 6 oz

500 ml/18 fl oz Sorbet syrup (see page 168)

1 tbsp apricot jam, sieved

Serves 8

Preparation time: 35 minutes

Cooking time: 30 minutes

· PREPARATION ·

Preheat the oven to 200°C/400°F/gas 7.

Preparing the base: On a lightly floured surface, roll out the pastry into a circle about 3 mm/⅛ in thick. Lightly grease the flan ring, place on the baking sheet, then line it with the pastry. You will be left with about 60 g/2 oz trimmings.

With your fingertips, lightly pinch up the edges of the pastry to form a little crest. Crimp diagonally all round the edge with a pastry crimper, or simply use your thumb and forefinger to shape the pastry. Chill for 20 minutes.

Filling: Mix together the two creams and spread them evenly over the chilled pastry base.

Cooking the base: Bake in the preheated oven for 30 minutes. When you remove the tart from the oven, leave it in the flan ring and on the baking sheet for about 10 minutes. Once it has cooled, remove the ring and transfer to a wire rack.

Preparing the oranges: Using a cannelizing knife, peel off about 12 long strips of zest at regular intervals from top to bottom of the oranges, then cut the oranges in half vertically.

Place the fruit on a board, cut side down and, with a fine serrated knife, cut into very fine, neat slices, about 2 mm/¹/₁₂ in thick. Spread them in a single layer in a deep dish. Bring the sorbet syrup to the boil and pour it over the orange slices. Cover with non-absorbent greaseproof paper, so that the fruit is thoroughly steeped in syrup.

Leave for about 30 minutes, until the syrup is completely cold, then carefully drain the orange slices and reserve the syrup.

Garnishing the tart: Arrange the orange slices in a spiral shape, starting from the outside of the tart (see the picture on page 86).

If you like, you can stand a few orange segments upright in the centre of the tart; cut the bases so that they stand firmly to give a very attractive effect.

Glazing: Mix 6 tablespoons of the reserved syrup with the apricot jam. Reduce by two-thirds over high heat, then carefully and evenly brush the glaze over the orange slices, taking care not to displace them.

· TO SERVE ·

Present the tart whole to your guests, then take it back to the kitchen and slice it with a serrated knife or a ham knife, taking care not to disarrange the oranges. The tart should be served at room temperature; on no account chill it before serving.

TARTE AUX PERLES DE GROSEILLES

(Tart with redcurrant pearls)

PICTURE PAGES 82-3

The colours of this unusual tart are stunning.

· PREPARATION ·

Preheat the oven to 220°C/425°F/gas 8.

Preparing the base: On a lightly floured surface, roll out the pastry to a thickness of about 3 mm/⅛ in. Grease the flan ring, place it on the baking sheet and line with the pastry. You will have about 60 g/2 oz trimmings left over.

Place a circle of greaseproof paper inside the pastry and fill with baking beans. Bake blind in the preheated oven for 20 minutes. Remove the baking beans with a spoon and lift out the paper. Set aside at room temperature. Lower the oven temperature to 180°C/350°F/gas 5.

The filling: In a bowl, whisk together the eggs, cream and sugar. Add the seeds from the split vanilla pod or the vanilla essence.

Baking the filled tart: Pour the filling into the part-baked tart case. Bake at 180°C/350°F/gas 5 for about 30 minutes, until the filling is set. Remove the flan ring before the tart has cooled completely.

The redcurrants: Remove the redcurrants from their stalks by sliding the prongs of a fork right down the stalk. Discard any damaged berries and place the rest in a bowl. Leave the white currants on their stalks.

Scatter the prepared redcurrants over the surface of the flan, so that they cover the entire surface and come right up to the top of the crust.

Glazing: Gently melt the redcurrant jelly and leave to cool. When it is almost cold, use a spoon to apply an even coating of glaze to the redcurrants. Decorate the tart with the white currants. You could, for example, use them to mark out each portion (see photo, pages 82-3).

· TO SERVE ·

Slide the tart on to a round serving plate and serve it whole, leaving your guests to help themselves. If you like, offer each guest a glass dish of vanilla ice cream. Its subtle, luscious richness and tiny speckles of black vanilla will complement the tart beautifully and offset its sharp flavour.

· INGREDIENTS ·

360 g/12 oz *Pâte sablée* (see page 47)

Pinch of flour

Butter, for greasing

CREAM FILLING:

4 eggs

440 ml/16 fl oz double cream

135 g/4½ oz sugar

½ vanilla pod, split *or* a few drops of pure vanilla essence

700 g/1 lb 8 oz redcurrants

60 g/2 oz white currants, to garnish (optional)

180 g/6 oz (about 6 tbsp) redcurrant jelly

Serves 8

Preparation time: 30 minutes

Cooking time: 50 minutes

· EQUIPMENT ·

Wooden or marble pastry board

1 flan ring, 22 cm/8½ in diameter, 4 cm/1½ in deep, or a loose-bottomed flan tin

Greaseproof paper

Baking beans

1 baking sheet

1 small saucepan

TARTE AL' COLOCHE

· INGREDIENTS ·

350 g/12 oz *Pâte Brisée*
(see page 31)

Pinch of flour

20 g/1 tbsp butter, for
greasing

12 medium dessert
apples, preferably Cox's

½ cinnamon stick or a
pinch of ground
cinnamon

4 turns of the pepper
mill (about 5 g/¾ tsp)

100 g/3½ oz butter

150 g/5 oz sugar

100 ml of double cream

2 eggs

Serves 8

Preparation time: 40
minutes

Cooking time: 45 minutes

This tart takes its name from the bubbling caramel, which puffs up and *coloche* (bubbles). It makes a divine winter pudding — creamy and delicate, with the apples all coated in caramel. Christian Germain, the *chef patron* of the Chateau de Montreuil in France, makes the best *tarte al' coloche* in the world!

· PREPARATION ·

Preheat the oven to 220°C/425°F/gas 8.

The pastry base: On a lightly floured surface, roll out the pastry to a thickness of about 3 mm/⅛ in.

Grease the flan ring and place it on a baking sheet. Line the whole ring with pastry, cutting off any excess with a sharp knife. Lightly crimp up the edges of the pastry to form a sort of frill above the edge of the ring.

Leave to rest in the fridge for 20 minutes before baking.

The apples: Peel, quarter and core them.

Place 4 quartered apples in a saucepan with 2 tablespoons water and the cinnamon. Cover the pan and cook gently until soft. Remove the cinnamon stick and add the pepper. Beat vigorously until they have the consistency of a compote. Set aside at room temperature.

Baking blind: Line the base and sides of the pastry with greaseproof paper. Fill with baking beans and bake in the preheated oven for 20 minutes.

As soon as the pastry is half-cooked, remove the beans and paper and leave the base in a warm place.

Reduce the oven temperature to 200°C/400°F/gas 7.

In a large, thick-bottomed pan, melt the butter, then immediately add the sugar. Cook gently until it becomes a very pale caramel. Add the remaining apple quarters and roll them in the caramel for 4 minutes. They should be cooked but still firm. Set aside in a cool place.

· ASSEMBLING THE TART ·

Spread the apple compote over the base of the tart, then arrange the quarters on top. Pour the remaining caramel into a bowl and stir in the cream and eggs. Beat together lightly, then pour the mixture over the apples.

Bake the tart at 200°C/400°F/gas 7 for 25 minutes.

· TO SERVE ·

Serve the tart warm and cut it at the table. Sprinkle lightly with icing sugar if you like.

· EQUIPMENT ·

Marble or wooden pastry
board

1 flan ring, 24 cm/9½ in
diameter, 3.5 cm/1½ in deep

Baking sheet

1 saucepan

Thick-bottomed pan

Greaseproof paper

Baking beans

PICTURE PAGE 77

CLAFOUTIS AUX CERISES
(Cherry clafoutis)

· INGREDIENTS ·

220 g/8 oz *Pâte brisée*
(see page 31)

2 pinches of flour

30 g/1 oz butter, for
greasing

500 g/1 lb 1 oz very ripe
black cherries

120 ml/4 fl oz milk

120 ml/4 fl oz double
cream

½ vanilla pod, split

4 eggs

170 g/6 oz sugar

2 drops orange blossom
water or a little Kirsch
(optional)

30 g/1 oz granulated
sugar

Serves 8

Preparation time: 30
minutes

Cooking time: 45 minutes

When we were children, our mother used to make this very easy dessert for us as a treat (and she still does!). In winter, pears or apples can be used instead of the cherries.

· PREPARATION ·

Preheat the oven to 220°C/425°F/gas 8.

The pastry case: On a lightly floured surface, roll out the pastry into a circle about 2-3 mm/⅛ in thick.

Lightly grease the flan tin, place on a baking sheet, then line it with the pastry. Roll the rolling pin over the top edge of the tin to cut off the excess pastry. You will have about 40 g/1½ oz trimmings. Leave to rest in the fridge for about 20 minutes.

Line the whole surface of the pastry with greaseproof paper and fill with baking beans.

Baking blind: Bake in the preheated oven for 20 minutes. Use a spoon to lift out the baking beans and remove the greaseproof paper. Keep at room temperature.

Reduce the oven temperature to 200°C/400°F/gas 7.

The cherries: Remove the stalks and stone the cherries, using a small piece of wire bent back at one end to make a loop; you should be able to remove the stones without cutting open the fruit.

The mixture: Combine the milk, cream and vanilla pod in a saucepan and boil for 1 minute.

In a bowl, whisk the eggs and sugar until light and frothy. Add a pinch of flour.

Discard the vanilla pod and pour the milk mixture on to the eggs, whisking lightly. Stir in the orange blossom water or Kirsch, if you are using it. Leave the mixture in a cool place, stirring from time to time.

Filling and cooking the pastry case: Arrange the cherries in the pastry case and pour over the mixture, which should still be slightly warm. Bake immediately at 200°C/400°F/gas 7 for 25 minutes.

As soon as the dessert is cooked, remove the side of the flan tin, leaving the *clafoutis* on the bottom.

· TO SERVE ·

Sprinkle the top of the *clafoutis* with granulated sugar just before serving. Serve the dessert while it is still warm so that the full flavour of the cherries comes through.

· EQUIPMENT ·

Wooden or marble pastry
board

1 loose-bottomed flan tin or
flan ring,
24 cm/9 in diameter,
2 cm/¾ in deep

Greaseproof paper

Baking beans

1 baking sheet

1 saucepan

1 bowl

COLD DESSERTS AND SWEETS

*A*ny number of cold sweets and desserts can be prepared in advance to make life easier for the cook — but make sure they are served chilled and not tepid.

Some desserts like *sablés* or *feuilletés* cannot be finally assembled until the last moment.

Almost all the recipes in this chapter are prepared with fruit, which lends a delicate texture and flavour to our desserts.

Most of these recipes can be frozen without harming their flavour or appearance, so why not prepare two or three desserts at the same time? Then, if you issue a last-minute invitation, you will have a delicious home-made dessert to offer your guests. We have indicated in each recipe whether or not it is suitable for freezing.

FEUILLETES AUX FRAMBOISES OU AUX FRAISES
(Raspberry or strawberry feuilletés)

· INGREDIENTS ·

400 g/14 oz raspberries
or strawberries

600 ml/1 pt red Fruit
coulis (see page 71)

500 ml/18 fl oz double
cream

50-100 ml/2-3 fl oz
Sorbet syrup (see
page 168), depending on
the tartness of the fruit,
well chilled

60 g/2 oz icing sugar

350 g/12 oz Puff pastry
(see pages 42-3)

· PREPARATION ·

The raspberries or strawberries: Wash the fruit, hull if necessary and, if you are using strawberries, halve or quarter them, depending on their size. Mix them in a bowl with about 300 ml/11 fl oz red fruit *coulis* and keep in the fridge.

The double cream: In a well-chilled bowl, whip the cream until it forms a ribbon. Add the chilled syrup and whip until almost stiff. Chill in the fridge, together with the piping bag and nozzle.

The puff pastry: Preheat the oven to 220°C/425°F/gas 8.

Dust the pastry board with icing sugar, not with flour, and roll out the pastry to a thickness of about 4 mm/⅛ in. Cut out 8 circles with the pastry cutter and place them on a baking sheet brushed with cold water. Leave to rest in a cold place for 20 minutes before baking.

· TO BAKE ·

Bake the circles in the preheated oven for about 10 minutes.

· EQUIPMENT ·

1 well-chilled bowl

Wooden *or* marble pastry
board

1 plain round pastry cutter,
9 cm/3½ in diameter

1 baking sheet

Piping bag, with a medium
plain or ridged nozzle

Wire rack

PICTURE PAGE 99

Serves 4

Preparation time: 25 minutes

Cooking time: 10 minutes

The icing sugar from the pastry board will have given the tops an attractive glaze. Use a palette knife to transfer the circles to a wire rack.

· TO SERVE ·

Using a small, sharp knife, make a small cavity in the centre of 4 of the pastry circles. Spread a little of the whipped cream over the bottom of each cavity, then fill generously with raspberries or strawberries. Pipe a pretty border of whipped cream around the rim of each filled circle, then top with the second pastry circle. Place on individual plates, pour a ribbon of fruit *coulis* around each *feuilleté* and pipe a little rosette of whipped cream on top of each one. Decorate with a raspberry or strawberry.

· NOTES ·

Never bake the pastry for these light, delicate, crisp *feuilletés* more than an hour or two before serving, and fill them at the very last moment. They are also delicious filled with wild strawberries. The sorbet syrup can be replaced by 50-100 g/2-4 oz icing sugar, depending on the tartness of the fruit.

ROULE MARQUIS
(Chocolate roulade with raspberries)

· INGREDIENTS ·

3 egg yolks

175 g/6 oz icing sugar

4 egg whites

50 g/2 oz cocoa powder

15 g/2 tsp potato flour *or* cornflour

1 tsp butter

Pinch of flour

250 ml/9 fl oz single cream

250 ml/9 fl oz red Fruit *coulis* (see page 71)

2 tbsp *framboise* liqueur (optional)

150 g/5 oz fresh raspberries

60 g/2 oz coffee liqueur beans (optional)

· PREPARATION ·

Preheat the oven to 200°C/400°F/gas 7.

The chocolate sponge: Beat together the egg yolks and 80 g/3 oz icing sugar until they form a ribbon.

Beat the egg whites until half-risen. Add 45 g/1½ oz icing sugar and beat at high speed for 1 minute until very stiff.

Using a flat slotted spoon, mix one-third of the egg whites into the yolks and stir until completely blended. Very carefully tip in the remaining egg whites all at once and mix gently.

Before the mixture becomes completely homogenous, sift in the cocoa and potato flour or cornflour, folding all the time. As soon as the mixture is well blended, stop folding, or it will become heavy.

Line a baking sheet with baking parchment or lightly buttered and floured greaseproof paper. Using a palette knife, spread the roulé mixture evenly over the paper to make a rectangle about 26 × 30 cm/10 × 12 in and 1.5 cm/½ in thick.

Bake in the preheated oven for 8-10 minutes. The top of the sponge should feel springy when pressed with the fingertips.

· EQUIPMENT ·

Electric mixer

Baking sheet

Baking parchment *or* greaseproof paper

Wire rack

1

Remove the cooked sponge from the oven and cover with a tea towel.

2

Immediately invert it on to a wire rack, so that the tea towel covers the rack. Carefully peel off the greaseproof paper.

1

2

3

Brush the sponge with a mixture of framboise liqueur and fruit coulis.

4

Scatter over the raspberries and then the coffee liqueur beans.

3

4

5

Using the tea towel to help you, roll up the filled sponge like a Swiss roll. Chill for 2-3 hours before serving.

6

After chilling, serve the roulé cut into diagonal slices. Dredge each slice with icing sugar and serve on chilled plates. Serve the reserved coulis separately.

5

6

Serves 6
Preparation time: 20 minutes
Cooking time: 8-10 minutes

If it is not sufficiently cooked, it will stick to the cloth after baking.

Remove from the oven and immediately invert the sponge onto a wire rack covered with a tea towel. Carefully peel off the paper, then leave in a cool place for 5-10 minutes.

The filling: Whip the cream with the remaining icing sugar until it forms a ribbon. Mix together the *framboise* liqueur and the fruit *coulis*. Brush the sponge with a quarter of the *coulis*. Reserve the rest to serve separately.

Trim the edges of the sponge with a knife, cutting off any slightly overcooked or dry parts.

Continued on page 100

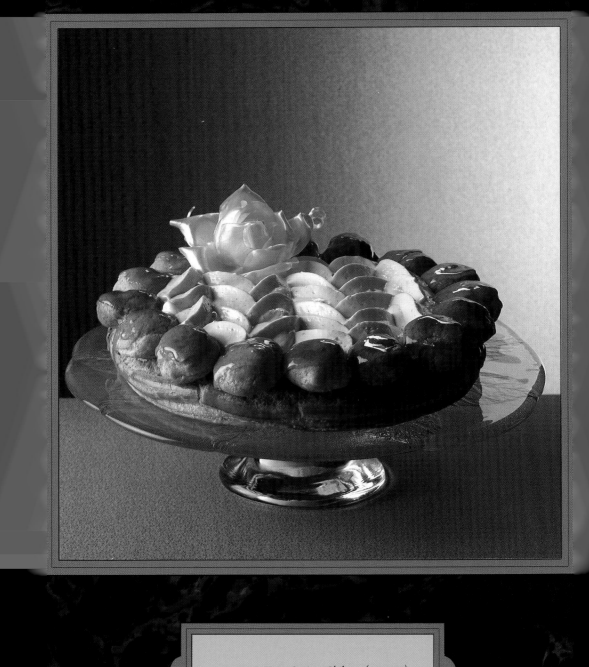

ABOVE *St Honoré, crème Chiboust (page 100)*

TOP LEFT *Pêches au champagne (page 109)*
TOP RIGHT *Nougat glacé au miel et aux figues de Provence (page 118)*
ABOVE *Feuilleté aux framboises (page 95)*

Using a palette knife, spread the whipped cream to within 1.5 cm/½ in of the edges of the sponge. Scatter over the raspberries and coffee liqueur beans.

Using the tea towel to help you, roll up the sponge like a Swiss roll. Chill in the fridge for 2-3 hours before serving.

· TO SERVE ·

Cut into diagonal slices. Dredge with icing sugar and serve on very cold plates. Serve the remaining fruit *coulis* separately in a sauceboat.

· NOTES ·

This luscious, light dessert can be made in advance and refrigerated for up to 24 hours. Use strawberries when raspberries are not available. The raspberry liqueur is not essential, but it does bring out the flavour of the fruit beautifully.

Coffee liqueur granules are available from specialist foodshops and add a delicious crunch to the filling.

ST. HONORE,
CREME CHIBOUST
(St. Honoré with crème Chiboust)

· INGREDIENTS ·

220 g/8 oz puff pastry trimmings *or* *Feuilletage minute* (see page 43)

Pinch of flour

1 quantity *Pâte à choux*, about 250 ml/9 fl oz (see page 46)

Eggwash made with 1 egg yolk and 1 tbsp milk

30 g/1 oz butter

200 g/7 oz sugar

1 quantity *Crème Chiboust* (see page 62)

· PREPARATION ·

Rolling out the base: On a lightly floured surface, roll out the pastry, turning it one-quarter turn after each roll, so that it becomes a neat circle about 26 cm/10 in diameter. The base will be 24 cm/9½ in diameter, so allow an extra couple of centimetres.

Decorating the base with the choux buns: Roll the pastry round the rolling pin, then unroll it onto a baking sheet which has been lightly brushed with cold water.

Using a *Pithiviers* marker or flan circle, cut out a 24 cm/9½ in pastry circle. Prick with the prongs of a fork.

Using the piping bag fitted with the 1.2 cm/½ in nozzle, pipe out the choux paste in a spiral shape, starting from the centre of the pastry base and pressing the nozzle down lightly onto the pastry. Stop piping about 3 cm/1¼ in from the edge of the pastry base.

Brush the exposed pastry border with eggwash, then pipe a 'crown' of choux paste all round the edge. This time, do not press down with the nozzle. Brush the 'crown' with eggwash, then leave to rest in a cool place for 30 minutes.

Lightly butter the other baking sheet, then pipe out 18

· EQUIPMENT ·

Wooden or marble pastry board

2 baking sheets

Piping bag

1 plain 1.2 cm/½ in nozzle

1 plain 0.5 cm/¼ in nozzle

1 St. Honoré *nozzle*, or a fluted 1.5-2 cm/¾ in nozzle

Wire rack

1 saucepan

1 × 24 cm/9½ in flan ring or Pithiviers *marker*

PICTURE PAGE 98

Serves 8

Preparation time: 35 minutes

Cooking time: 35 minutes for the base, 20 minutes for the choux buns

small choux buns, about 2 cm/¾ in diameter. Brush with eggwash and press lightly with the back of a fork.

· TO COOK ·

Preheat the oven to 220°C/425°F/gas 8.

Bake the buns and base for 10 minutes, then lower the temperature to 200°C/400°F/gas 7 and cook the small buns for a further 10 minutes and the base for a further 25 minutes.

Transfer the cooked buns and base to a wire rack and leave to cool at room temperature.

· ASSEMBLING THE ST. HONORE ·

In a saucepan, cook the sugar with 3 tbsp water until it turns pale amber.

Make a small hole in the bottom of the choux buns with the point of a knife. Insert the point of a small knife in the base of the buns and dip the tops into the caramelized sugar. Place on a baking sheet and leave to cool. As soon as they are cold, fill the buns through the hole in the bottom with the *crème Chiboust*, using the very small nozzle.

Arrange the filled buns evenly on top of the 'crown', sticking them down with a little caramel.

Using the special large nozzle, fill the centre of the *St. Honoré* with the *crème Chiboust*, piping it into an attractive pattern (see photo, page 98), or use the fluted nozzle to make rosettes, if you prefer.

· TO SERVE ·

Leave the *St. Honoré* in a cold place for at least 2 hours before serving. Serve on a round plate and cut it at the table. Garnish the dessert with a sugar or marzipan flower for a very pretty effect. A few wild strawberries or raspberries scattered over the cream just before serving are as good to look at as they are to taste.

· NOTES ·

You can use *crème Chantilly* (see page 66) instead of the *crème Chiboust*, but do not fill the choux buns, as the cream will melt the caramel when you stick them to the 'crown'.

1
After baking, invert the sponge and, when cool, peel off the paper.

2
Cut out 2 long bands the width of the flan rings.

3
Cut 1 circle the same diameter as the rings.

4
Place the circles on the cake boards inside the flan rings. Line each ring with a sponge band, cutting 1 band in half to fill the gaps.

5
After filling each mould one-quarter full of the mixture, scatter over a quarter of the fruit.

6
Pour in enough mixture to cover the fruit; it should come about two-thirds up the moulds. Scatter in the remaining fruit and top with more mixture.

7
Top with the daisy-shaped circles and press down gently.

8
After chilling, remove the ring and serve sliced.

CHARLOTTE AUX POIRES ET FRAISES DES BOIS

(Pear and wild strawberry charlotte)

· INGREDIENTS ·

400 g/14 oz fresh *or* canned pears in syrup, drained and cut into 7 mm/¼ in cubes

50 g/2 oz powdered milk

125 ml/4 fl oz milk

12 egg yolks

100 g/3½ oz sugar

3 quantities Sponge biscuit mixture (see recipe 2, page 53)

750 ml/1¼ pt whipping cream

200 ml/7 fl oz Sorbet syrup (see page 168)

400 ml/14 fl oz white pear liqueur

9 leaves of gelatine

1 quantity *Meringue italienne* (see page 58)

150 g/5 oz wild strawberries *or* raspberries

icing sugar, to serve

600 ml/1 pt red Fruit *coulis* (see page 71)

Makes 2 charlottes, each serving 10

Preparation time: 1 hour, plus 3-5 hours chilling

· PREPARATION ·

The crème anglaise: Purée 40 g/1½ oz of the pears and place in a saucepan with the powdered and fresh milk. Beat together lightly. Bring the mixture to the boil.

In a bowl, whisk together the egg yolks and sugar until they form a light ribbon.

Stirring constantly, pour on the boiling milk mixture, then pour the mixture back into the saucepan. Poach gently, stirring continuously, until the custard is thick enough to coat a wooden spoon, like a normal *crème anglaise*.

Pass the custard through a conical strainer into a bowl and set aside.

The sponge: Pipe out diagonally a sponge rectangle 60 × 40 cm/23½ × 16 in (see step-by-step instructions, opposite); this will make the 2 bases.

Pipe out 2 sponge rounds about the same diameter as the flan rings (20 cm/8 in), piping them in a sort of daisy shape. These will be the tops.

Cook the sponges; once cooked, they should be about 1.5 cm/½ in thick.

The cream: Beat until it forms a ribbon. Set aside.

Cutting out the sponge: Turn over the sponge rectangle. Carefully remove the greaseproof paper, then trim the edges with a serrated knife. Using the side of a flan ring as a guide, cut out 2½ bands from the long edge of the rectangle, then a circle the same diameter as the flan ring. With the serrated knife, slice the circle horizontally in half.

Place the 2 sponge bases on the cake boards and put the flan rings on top. Mix together the syrup and one-third of the pear liqueur and brush the sponge with this mixture. Brush the 2½ bands of sponge with the mixture.

Line each flan ring with a band of sponge, cutting the half band to fill the gaps.

Assembling the charlottes: Soak the gelatine leaves in very cold water for 15 minutes, then drain.

In a saucepan, heat the remaining liqueur until tepid. Drain the gelatine well, then stir it into the tepid pear liqueur with the pan off the heat.

Using a wire whisk, fold two-thirds of the *meringue italienne* into the whipped cream. Do not overwork. Do the same with the *crème anglaise*, which should be almost cold. Mix until completely homogenous. With a spatula, stir in the tepid pear

· EQUIPMENT ·

2 stainless steel flan rings, 20 cm/8 in diameter, 6 cm/2¼ in deep

1 saucepan

Conical strainer

2 × 22 cm/8½ in round cake boards

Piping bag, with a plain 1 cm/½ nozzle

liqueur and gelatine mixture.

Using a ladle, fill each flan ring one-quarter full of the mixture. Scatter a quarter of the pear cubes and the wild strawberries over each charlotte. Pour in enough mixture to cover the fruit; it should come about two-thirds up the moulds. Scatter in the rest of the fruit, fill up the moulds with mixture and place the 2 'daisy' circles on top, pressing down gently so that they stick to the *bavaroise* mixture.

Place in the fridge for 5 hours, or freeze for 3 hours before serving.

· TO SERVE ·

Carefully remove the flan ring. Sprinkle the top of the dessert with icing sugar. Serve very cold, in slices, accompanied by a red fruit *coulis*.

· STORAGE ·

The charlottes will keep for 2 or 3 days in the fridge or for up to a week in the freezer, wrapped in clingfilm.

· NOTES ·

It is always best to cook the sponge the day before so that it does not crumble when you cut it.

It is not really possible to reduce the quantities successfully for this recipe, which is why we suggest you make 2 charlottes, each for 10 people. You must also make a full quantity of *meringue italienne* and discard the remainder, or keep it for another use.

The wild strawberries are not absolutely essential, but they are wonderfully delicate and flavoursome. However, raspberries can be substituted.

OEUFS A LA NEIGE AUX COPEAUX DE CHOCOLAT

(Snow eggs with chocolate curls)

· INGREDIENTS ·

6 egg whites
340 g/11 oz sugar
250 ml/9 fl oz *Crème anglaise*, well-flavoured with vanilla (see page 70)
8 Chocolate curls (see page 242)
METHOD 1:
30 g/1 oz butter
1 tbsp oil, for greasing
METHOD 2:
1 lt/1¾ pt milk
60 g/2 oz sugar
1 tbsp oil, for greasing

Serves 4
Preparation time: 25 minutes
Cooking time: 6 minutes, plus making the caramel

This delicious dessert can be made even more delectable by serving some strawberries or raspberries in a separate bowl.

· PREPARATION ·

Beat the egg whites until soft peaks form, then, still beating, add 130 g/4 oz sugar and beat until very firm.

Method 1: Preheat the oven to 140°C/275°F/gas 2. To make attractive 'snowballs', pipe the beaten egg whites into the lightly buttered tartlet tins, using a piping bag without a nozzle. Smooth over the surface with a palette knife so that the balls are smooth and even. Cook in the preheated oven for 10 minutes, then carefully unmould the balls onto lightly greased foil or a greased baking sheet.

Method 2: In a shallow pan, heat the milk and 60 g/2 oz sugar to about 90°C/194°F. Keep at a very gentle simmer.

Using a large kitchen spoon, form the beaten whites into 4 *quenelles*, about the size of a large egg, smoothing the surface carefully with a palette knife. Gently lower each into the simmering milk, rinsing the spoon in cold water between each operation.

Poach for 3 minutes, then turn over the *quenelles* and poach for a further 3 minutes. With a slotted spoon, transfer the *quenelles* to drain on a tea towel. They should be just firm to the touch, but still light and delicate.

As soon as the *quenelles* have cooled and drained, arrange them on lightly greased foil or a greased baking sheet.

· CARAMELIZING THE 'SNOWBALLS' ·

Place the remaining 210 g/7 oz sugar in a saucepan or preserving pan and set over low heat, stirring continuously. As soon as the sugar caramelizes to a light golden colour, spoon it generously over the poached egg whites.

· TO SERVE ·

Divide the well-chilled *crème anglaise* between 4 shallow soup plates. Place 1 *quenelle* or 2 snowballs in each dish and arrange a chocolate curl at either edge.

· NOTES ·

Once they have been coated with caramel, the egg whites tend to become slightly moist and the caramel is no longer crunchy, so it is best to eat them within an hour or two.

· EQUIPMENT ·

Electric mixer, or mixing bowl and whisk
1 saucepan or preserving pan
Baking sheet or aluminium foil
METHOD 1:
Piping bag
8 tartlet tins, 7 cm/3 in at the top, 5.5 cm/2¼ in at the base, 1.5 cm/½ in deep
METHOD 2:
1 large shallow pan
1 large kitchen spoon, 10 cm/4 in long, 7 cm/2¼ in wide, 3 cm/1¼ in deep

PICTURE PAGE 106

TOP *Sablé aux fraises (page 137)*
BOTTOM *Oeufs à la neige aux copeaux de chocolat (page 105)*

TOP *Igloo douillet (page 108)*
BOTTOM *Palmerosa de mon ami Valentin*
(page 129)

IGLOO DOUILLET
(Cosy igloos)

· INGREDIENTS ·

1 quantity Sponge
biscuit mixture, recipe 1
(see page 53)

200 g/7 oz redcurrant
jelly

1½ leaves of gelatine

75 g/2½ oz sultanas

300 ml/11 fl oz white
dessert wine (preferably
Beaumes de Venise)

½ vanilla pod

3 egg yolks

10 g/1½ tsp custard
powder

Juice of ½ lemon

1 tbsp double cream

1 quantity *Meringue
italienne* (see page 58)

½ quantity *Crème
anglaise* (see page 70)

1 tbsp Marie Brizard
liqueur

Serves 8

Preparation time: 50
minutes

Cooking time: about 6
minutes

· PREPARATION ·

Preheat the oven to 220°C/425°F/gas 8.

The sponge biscuit: Spread the prepared mixture into a rectangular shape, 20 × 30 cm/8 × 12 in, on a baking sheet lined with baking parchment or greased greaseproof paper. It should be 3-5 mm/⅛-¼ in thick. Any remaining mixture (there should be about one-third left) can be used for making sponge fingers or small biscuits.

Bake in the preheated oven for about 6 minutes.

Cover with a tea towel and invert onto a flat surface. Peel off the paper and spread the redcurrant jelly over the sponge. Using the tea towel to help you, roll up the sponge like a Swiss roll, as small as possible, about 2 cm/¾ in diameter. Leave to settle in the fridge for several hours or place in the freezer, which will make it easier to slice.

The gelatine: Soak in very cold water for 15 minutes, then drain.

The sultanas: Blanch in boiling water, refresh, drain and place in a bowl. Pour over 50 ml/2 fl oz wine and leave the sultanas to macerate.

The wine custard: Put the remaining wine and the half vanilla pod in a saucepan and bring to the boil.

In a small bowl, combine the egg yolks and custard powder and beat with a small wire whisk until pale and frothy. Pour in the boiling wine, whisking continuously. Remove the vanilla.

Return the mixture to the saucepan and set over low heat, stirring continuously with a wooden spatula for 3-4 minutes, until the mixture is thick enough to coat the spatula.

Take the pan off the heat and stir in the drained gelatine. Immediately pass the custard through a conical strainer into a bowl. Set aside in a cool place, stirring from time to time to prevent a skin from forming.

Assembling the igloos: Cut the sponge roll into 3 mm/⅛ in slices and use them to line the moulds right to the top.

Stir in a few drops of lemon juice, the cream and half the *meringue italienne* into the wine custard (which should be barely lukewarm) and fill the moulds two-thirds full with this mixture. Divide the wine-soaked sultanas between the moulds, then fill to the top with custard.

Wrap each mould in clingfilm or greaseproof paper and chill in the fridge for several hours.

· TO SERVE ·

Unmould the igloos onto well-chilled serving plates. Flavour

· EQUIPMENT ·

1 baking sheet

1 saucepan

Conical strainer

8 hemispherical moulds,
preferably stainless steel,
9 cm/3½ in diameter,
5 cm/2 in deep, 4.5 cm/1¾ in
at the base

Greaseproof paper or baking
parchment

PICTURE PAGE 107

the *crème anglaise* with Marie Brizard and pour a few spoonfuls around each igloo. Enhance the presentation with some spun sugar Angel's Hair (see page 221) scattered over the igloos to look like fallen stalactites, or add a delicate, childlike note by floating a few flakes of rose-coloured meringue onto the *crème anglaise*.

· NOTES ·

Although you will use only two-thirds of the sponge biscuit mixture, you must make a full quantity in order to obtain a very light texture. The same applies to the *meringue italienne*. Keep the remaining half quantity for another use.

You can prepare this pudding at least 24 hours in advance, but unmould and garnish the igloos at the last moment.

P E C H E S   A U   C H A M P A G N E
(Peaches poached in champagne)

· INGREDIENTS ·

4 very ripe peaches, preferably white

500 ml/18 fl oz dry champagne

350 ml/12 fl oz Sorbet syrup (see page 168)

1 small vanilla pod

250 g/9 oz strawberries

150 g/5 oz sugar

250 ml/9 fl oz double cream

Juice of ½ lemon

4 small sprigs of fresh mint

Serves 4

Preparation time: 20 minutes

Cooking time: about 8 minutes

· EQUIPMENT ·

1 shallow pan

1 sieve or blender

1 bowl

PICTURE PAGE 99

This very quick and easy dessert needs to be tasted to be fully appreciated.

· PREPARATION ·

The peaches: Make a very light incision all round the peach skins. Plunge the peaches into boiling water, then into cold water and peel. Place them in a shallow pan, pour over the champagne and syrup and add the vanilla pod. Bring slowly to the boil over low heat and poach the peaches at about 85°C/185°F. If the peaches are very ripe, they will be poached after 5 minutes.

Keep them in a cool place in the syrup, but do not refrigerate. Drain the peaches, reserving the poaching liquid.
The strawberries: Hull them and purée in a blender, or rub though a fine sieve set over a bowl. Stir the sugar into the purée.

Whip the cream until it forms a ribbon, then stir in the strawberry purée and the lemon juice.

· TO SERVE ·

Serve the peaches on round plates, or in glass dishes or small bowls. Line the bottom of the dishes with the strawberry cream and arrange a cooled but not chilled peach on top. Garnish each peach with a sprig of mint.

Serve the chilled poaching liquid separately in a sauceboat; it complements the strawberry cream beautifully.

TOP LEFT *Délice au cassis (page 131)*
BOTTOM LEFT *Rozenn au parfum d'orange
mentholé (page 112)*
ABOVE *Délice aux fruits de la passion (page 132)*

ROZENN AU PARFUM D'ORANGE MENTHOLE

(Chocolate and orange Rozenn with mint-flavoured sauce)

· INGREDIENTS ·

1 quantity *Meringue italienne* (see page 58)

280 g/10 oz bitter *couverture* chocolate, plus 90 g/3 oz Menier chocolate *or*

370 g/13 oz good quality bitter chocolate

125 g/4 oz butter, softened

1 orange-flavoured Sponge biscuit, 22 cm/8½ in diameter (see page 56)

4 tbsp Sorbet syrup (see page 168)

4 tbsp Grand Marnier

400 ml/14 fl oz double cream

400 ml/14 fl oz whipping cream

TOPPING:

280 g/10 oz plain chocolate covering *or* bitter *couverture*

CREME ANGLAISE:

6 egg yolks

80 g/3 oz sugar

500 ml/18 fl oz milk

25 g/1 oz fresh mint sprigs

Makes 2 cakes, each serving 8

Preparation time: 1½ hours

· PREPARATION ·

Shred the *couverture* and break the Menier chocolate into a bowl. Place in a bain-marie or double boiler and melt the chocolate. Immediately stir in the butter with a spatula, a little at a time, until it has all melted.

Using a serrated knife, slice the sponge biscuit horizontally into 4 circles of equal thickness. Brush each circle with a mixture of the syrup and Grand Marnier.

Place the flan rings on the cake boards and place 1 sponge circle in each. Set aside.

The cream: Whip the 2 creams until thick.

The chocolate mousse: Using a balloon whisk, carefully fold 85 per cent of the meringue into the melted chocolate. Add about one-third of this mixture to the cream and beat lightly together. Using a spatula, fold the remaining chocolate mixture into the cream and mix very lightly until the mixture is just amalgamated. Do not overwork the mixture, or it may separate.

Assembling the Rozenns: Pour 40 per cent of the mixture into each flan ring and smooth the surface with a palette knife.

Top with a sponge circle and press down lightly with your fingertips.

Divide the remaining chocolate mixture between the 2 cakes and level the surface with a palette knife until very smooth. Slide the knife between the table and the cake board and jiggle it up and down to tap out any air bubbles. Smooth over the top again.

Place the cakes in the fridge for a minimum of 4 hours, or in the freezer for 2 hours.

· TO DECORATE ·

Using a cloth or sponge dipped in very hot water then squeezed almost dry, press it around the edges of the flan rings which will effectively loosen the cakes. Then carefully lift off the flan rings.

Smooth over the sides with a palette knife to cover any gaps if necessary. Slide the palette knife under the cakes and transfer them to a wire rack set over a shallow dish.

Melt the chocolate covering or *couverture* and ladle it over the cakes to coat them completely; do not leave any part uncovered. Smooth the edges with a small knife if necessary. Place the cakes briefly in the fridge to harden before serving.

· EQUIPMENT ·

Double saucepan or *bain-marie*

Electric mixer

2 flan rings, 22 cm/8½ in diameter, 3.5 cm/1½ in deep

2 × 24 cm/9½ in round cake boards

1 sieve

PICTURE PAGE 110

Continued on page 114

1

Shred the couverture with a knife.

1

2

Brush the sliced sponge circles with the mixture of syrup and Grand Marnier.

2

3

Carefully fold 85 per cent of the meringue into the melted chocolate.

3

4

Now add one-third of the chocolate meringue mixture to the cream, then the remainder.

4

5

Pour 40 per cent of the chocolate mousse into each flan ring and smooth the surface. Place a sponge circle in each ring and press down lightly with your fingertips.

5

6

Divide the remaining mousse between the 2 cakes.

6

7

After chilling for at least 4 hours, carefully lift off the ring.

7

8

Place the cakes on a rack set over a dish. Melt the couverture or cake covering and ladle it over the cakes, covering them completely. Smooth the edges; chill until hardened.

8

· TO SERVE ·

The sauce: Make the *crème anglaise* according to the method on page 70, but using the quantities given in this recipe. Infuse the mint in the milk instead of the vanilla pod. Pass through a strainer, chill and serve very cold.

The cake: Serve it whole at the table and cut individual slices for your guests, using a knife dipped in hot water and wiped dry between each slice. Pour a ribbon of sauce around each slice. This mint-flavoured sauce accompanies the *Rozenn* superbly.

· STORAGE ·

This dessert freezes very successfully; leave it inside the flan ring and wrap in clingfilm. Pour over the coating just before serving. Since you cannot make a smaller quantity of sponge biscuit mixture without spoiling the quality, it is better to prepare 2 cakes at the same time and freeze one of them. They will keep in the freezer for up to 1 week.

As with all desserts containing *meringue italienne*, you need to make the full quantity to obtain a successful mixture; discard the remaining 15 per cent, or keep it for another use.

LE FRAISIER
(Strawberry gateau)

· INGREDIENTS ·

Double quantity Genoise sponge, (see page 60)

1 tbsp butter, for greasing

Pinch of flour

2 kg/4 lb 4 oz medium-sized strawberries

250 ml/9 fl oz Sorbet syrup (see page 168)

150 ml/5 fl oz Kirsch

Double quantity *Crème mousseline* (see page 63)

320 g/11 oz confectioners' almond paste

Green food colouring

Pinch of icing sugar

2 tbsp Royal icing (see page 236)

· PREPARATION ·

The genoise: Prepare the sponge according to the method on page 60 and bake in the lightly buttered and floured mould or tin for about 1 hour.

The strawberries: Wash them if necessary. If they are not gritty, simply wipe them, so that they retain their full flavour and texture. Keep 8 or 10 of the best strawberries aside for decoration and hull the rest.

Filling the sponge: Using a serrated knife or ham slicer, cut the cake in half horizontally. Brush the cut side of each slice with a mixture of syrup and Kirsch.

Place the bottom half of the cake on the baking sheet and, using a palette knife, cover it with half the *crème mousseline*. Lay the strawberries over the cream, keeping them close together and making sure that those on the outer edge of the cake are pointing inwards towards the centre. Cover with the remaining *crème mousseline* and lay the top of the cake on this. Press down lightly with your fingertips, then refrigerate the cake for at least 8 hours, but not more than 24 hours.

Decorating the dessert: Add green food colouring to the almond paste to achieve the desired effect, then roll it out as

· EQUIPMENT ·

1 Genoise mould or cake tin, 36 × 30 cm/14 × 12 in, 5 cm/2 in deep

1 × 40 cm/16in square cake board

1 baking sheet

Round or rectangular doilies

PICTURE PAGES 116-7

Serves 40

Preparation time: 1 hour 45 minutes, plus 8 hours chilling

Cooking time: 1 hour

evenly as possible on a surface lightly dusted with icing sugar. Roll it into a rectangle somewhat larger than the base of the cake (about 38 × 32 cm/15 × 12½ in). Roll the almond paste onto the rolling pin, then unroll it over the top of the cake. Trim the 4 sides with a serrated knife or ham slicer, taking care to wipe the blade each time. You should cut off about 1 cm/½ in all round, which will leave you with about 50 g/2 oz trimmings.

Use a large palette knife to slide the dessert onto the cake board base decorated with lace doilies.

Use a greaseproof cone to pipe out the word *Fraisier* in royal icing on top of the cake and pipe an attractive decorative border around the edge (see page 237).

· TO SERVE ·

The dessert is now ready to serve. Cut it into 5 slices widthways and 8 slices lengthways, giving 40 portions in all.

Garnish the cake with the reserved strawberries dipped in hard crack sugar or a red fruit *coulis*. (The recipe for the sugar is included in the *Croquembouche* recipe on page 126.)

· NOTES ·

Do not refrigerate the cake once it is coated with almond paste, as the paste will become moist.

If possible, bake the Genoise the previous day; it will then be easier to slice for filling.

This delicious dessert can be served with a red fruit *coulis* (see page 71). Allow 100 ml/3½ fl oz per person.

Le Fraisier (page 114)

TOP LEFT *Alméria (page 136)*
BOTTOM LEFT *L'assiette des trois sablés (page 138)*
ABOVE *Petit coeur de fromage blanc aux fruits rouges (page 119)*

Using a balloon whisk, carefully fold the whipped cream into the cooled *crème pâtissière*.

Assembling the charlottes: Divide the chocolate mixture between the 2 sponge-lined flan rings. Ladle over irregular quantities of the Grand Marnier mixture, letting it drop in spiral patterns to give a marbled effect. You must do this as soon as you have made the *bavaroises*, or the mixtures will set and you will not achieve the attractive marbling.

Place in the fridge for 4 hours, or in the freezer for 1½ hours.

· TO SERVE ·

Run a knife blade between the edge of the sponge and the inside of the flan ring and lift off the ring, rotating it slightly as you lift. Cut into slices with a knife dipped in hot water and serve very cold. A few chocolate curls (see page 242) make a pretty garnish for this dish, or accompany it with some Grand Marnier-flavoured *crème anglaise*, served in a sauceboat.

· STORAGE ·

If left in its flan ring and wrapped in clingfilm, one of the desserts can be kept in the fridge for 3 days, or for up to a week in the freezer.

1

2

1
After baking and cooling, invert the sponge and carefully peel off the paper, starting from one corner.

2
Cut out 3 long bands and 2 circles.

3
With the circles on the cake boards, line the rings with sponge bands, syrup side inwards. Cut strips from the third band to fill gaps. Trim the edges.

4
Pour the chocolate bavaroise into the rings, then quickly ladle in the Grand Marnier bavaroise to give a marbled effect.

3

4

Croquembouche (page 126)

CROQUEMBOUCHE

1.1 kg/2 lb 6 oz
Nougatine (see page 233)

2 tbsp peanut oil

2 tbsp Royal icing (see
page 236)

400 ml/14 fl oz Choux
paste (see below)

450 ml/16 fl oz double
cream, well chilled

950 g/2 lb *Crème
pâtissière* (see page 61)

50 ml/2 fl oz Kirsch
(optional)

750 g/1 lb 10 oz sugar

100 g/3½ oz glucose

10-12 sugar roses (see
pages 226-7) (optional)

CHOUX PASTE:

160 g/5½ oz butter

200 ml/8 fl oz water

200 ml/8 fl oz milk

¾ tsp fine salt

1½ tsp sugar

240 g/8 oz flour

7 × 70 g/size 1 eggs

Makes 1 Croquembouche
60 cm/24 in high, made
with 110 choux buns
Serves 25–30

A *Croquembouche* is the traditional centrepiece for christenings, first communions and weddings in France. You can make it more or less impressive, depending on the number of choux buns you use.

· PREPARATION ·

The nougatine: This must be divided into 4 pieces of the following weights: 770 g/1 lb 11 oz, 130 g/4 oz, and 2 pieces each of 100 g/3½ oz, but only take and work 1 piece at a time from the mass. Immediately roll out the first piece on a warm baking sheet or plastic board, keeping the rest of the *nougatine* warm in the oven or under a lamp.

First shaping: Roll out the 130 g/4 oz piece of *nougatine* to a thickness of 0.5 cm/¼ in. With a large knife, cut out 20 triangles 4 cm/1½ in at the base and 5 cm/2in high. Before they harden, drape them over the *tuile* shaper or the small rolling pin, so that they become slightly rounded. You will be left with about 30 g/1 oz trimmings.

Place the shaped triangles on a lightly oiled pastry sheet as soon as they have cooled.

Second shaping: Roll out one of the 100 g/3½ oz pieces of *nougatine* to a thickness of 0.5 cm/¼ in. Using the larger pastry cutter, cut out 5 half moons, 2.5 cm/1 in wide, and place them on the pastry sheet with the triangles.

You will be left with about 25 g/1 oz trimmings.

Third shaping: Roll out the second 100 g/3½ oz piece of *nougatine* to a thickness of 0.5 cm/¼ in and cut out one 11 cm/4½ in circle and one 7 cm/2¾ in circle with the pastry cutters. Place on the pastry sheet with the other shapes.

You will be left with about 45 g/1½ oz trimmings.

Fourth shaping: Roll the largest piece of *nougatine* into a circle 1 cm/⅓ in thick. Line the lightly oiled flan ring or sponge tin with this circle.

With a small, sharp knife, trim off the excess *nougatine* from the top of the mould, so that the edge is very smooth and even. As soon as the *nougatine* base has cooled, carefully unmould it and place it on the pastry sheet with the other shapes.

Take particular care with this shape, as it will form the base for the *Croquembouche*.

You will be left with about 120 g/4 oz trimmings

Decoration: Using a paper cone, decorate each shape with royal icing (see photo, page 237).

Set the *nougatine* base upside down on the cake board. Decorate all round the base with royal icing to hide any gaps

3 baking sheets

1 non-stick plastic board

Rolling pin, weighted or
made from heavy hardwood

Small rolling pin or tuile
shaper

2 plain or fluted pastry
cutters, 1 × 11 cm/4½ in
diameter, 1 × 7 cm/2¾ in
diameter

1 flan ring or sponge tin,
25 cm/10 in diameter,
5 cm/2 in deep

Greaseproof piping cornet

1 cake board,
27 cm/11 in diameter

Piping bag, fitted with a
plain 5 mm/¼ in nozzle

1 bowl

1 copper sugar pan

1 Croquembouche *mould*

Sugar thermometer

Sugar lamp (optional)

PICTURE PAGE 125

and to anchor the base onto the cake board.

The choux paste: Prepare and bake according to the recipe (page 46), using the piping bag fitted with a plain nozzle to pipe out 110 choux buns, about 2.5 cm/1 in diameter.

The light cream: Beat the double cream until it forms a ribbon, then fold in the *crème pâtissière*. Beat lightly until the creams are amalgamated, then flavour with Kirsch if required.

The sugar: Pour 250 ml/9 fl oz water into the sugar pan and add the sugar. Stir lightly with a skimmer and, when the sugar begins to dissolve, set the pan over moderate heat until the sugar has dissolved completely and begins to boil. Skim the surface, and brush down the inside of the pan, dipping the brush in cold water each time. Add the glucose and cook until the temperature reaches 160°C/320°F (very hard crack). It should be a very clear amber.

The choux buns: Using a small knife, make a small hole in the base of each bun. One by one, dip the tops into the sugar, to cover about one-third of each bun. Place on a lightly oiled baking sheet to cool. When the buns are quite cold, use the piping bag to fill them with the cream mixture.

Assembling the choux buns: This can be done 4-6 hours before serving.

Lightly oil the inside of the *Croquembouche* mould. Place one bun in the bottom of the mould, with the sugared side against the cone. Spear one bun with the point of a small knife and dip one-fifth of one edge in the sugar; place this bun against one side of the first bun, arranging it so that the sugared side is against the wall of the mould. The hot sugar will stick this bun to the first one.

Continue to add more buns in the same way, making only one row at a time, so that the rows remain straight.

The *Croquembouche* is assembled when all the buns have been used or the mould is full. Leave it for a few moments until the sugar is completely cold. Check that the mould is not sticking to the *Croquembouche* by rotating it slightly with your hand.

The finishing touches: Carefully invert the mould onto the *nougatine* base and remove the mould to reveal the pile of choux buns.

Using a little of the cooked sugar, stick the *nougatine* triangles around the base, arrange the half moons and circles at the top, and finish with the sugar roses.

Nougatine can be rather difficult to work, so you may find it easier to omit the triangles and other shapes, but the base is indispensable.

A few extra roses placed around the base will help to anchor the choux buns to the *nougatine*, and make the *Croquembouche* more stable. The sugar roses can be replaced by marzipan

1

5

PALMEROSA DE MON AMI VALENTIN

1

With a flexible knife, slice the peeled grapefruit into segments between the membranes. Squeeze the juice from the peel and pith, dice the flesh, and sprinkle over the sugar.

2

Cut the biscuit joconde in circles, place on a wire rack and brush with vanilla syrup.

2

3

Set the bowl of meringue in a bowl of crushed ice. Lightly whisk in the grapefruit juice mixture, then stir in the whipped cream.

3

4

4

Carefully fold in the diced grapefruit, taking care to separate the dice.

5

Stand the moulds in crushed ice. Spoon one-third of the grapefruit mixture into the moulds and spread it up the sides.

6

Cut a small triangle out of 8 sponge rounds, then make two cuts from the opposite side almost to the centre. Press one round into each mould.

6

7

Top the filled moulds with a sponge round. Smooth the surface and scrape off any excess mixture. Wrap in clingfilm and chill for 4 hours.

7

8

Unmould the chilled palmerosas and spoon over the strawberry glaze. Serve very cold.

8

flowers, which are easier to make — or even by coloured *dragées* placed here and there; these can look very pretty.

· TO SERVE ·

Using a knife with a rigid blade, first remove the *nougatine* 'crown', put it on a plate, and break it into 6 or 8 more or less equal pieces.

Starting from the top of the *Croquembouche*, slide the knife blade between the choux buns and serve 3 or 4 on to each plate. When everyone has been served, use the knife to break up part of the *nougatine* base, especially the decorative triangles. Pass around the plate of *nougatine* pieces for your guests to help themselves.

· NOTES ·

If the sugar cools and thickens while you are assembling the buns, heat it very gently over a low flame from time to time, but do not overheat it.

PALMEROSA DE MON AMI VALENTIN

· INGREDIENTS ·

5 grapefruit, preferably pink

50 g/2 oz sugar

1 baked *Biscuit joconde* (see page 55)

5 tbsp Sorbet syrup (see page 168), flavoured with vanilla

4½ leaves of gelatine

50 ml/2 fl oz Grand Marnier

350 ml/12 fl oz double cream, chilled

1 quantity *Meringue italienne* (see page 58)

FOR THE GLAZE:

3 leaves of gelatine

300 g/10 oz strawberries

150 g/5 oz sugar

½ quantity red Fruit coulis (see page 71)

48 raspberries

This recipe was given to me by a good friend and famous *pâtissier*, Monsieur Valentin. It takes a long time to prepare, but its subtle, sweet flavour and refreshing tang make it worthwhile.

· PREPARATION ·

The grapefruit: Using a supple-bladed knife, pare off the peel and pith, then cut the flesh into segments between the white membranes. Squeeze out all the juice from the peel and pulp into a bowl. Cut the grapefruit segments into medium dice, sprinkle over the sugar and mix gently. Place in a strainer set over the bowl containing the grapefruit juice and leave to drain for 30 minutes. Measure the resulting juices into a jug; you should have not more than 200 ml/7 fl oz. Strain the juices.

The biscuit joconde: Cut out sixteen 8 cm/3¼ in circles. Arrange them on a wire rack and brush lightly with the vanilla syrup.

The gelatine: Soak in very cold water for 15 minutes. Drain and place in a saucepan, together with one-third of the grapefruit juice and the Grand Marnier. Set over gentle heat to dissolve the gelatine; do not let the mixture boil. Stir in the

· EQUIPMENT ·

1 sieve

1 conical strainer

Crushed ice

1 small saucepan

1 pastry cutter, 8 cm/3¼ in diameter

8 round moulds or dishes, preferably stainless steel, 9 cm/3½ in diameter, 5 cm/2 in deep, 4.5 cm/1¼ in at the base

Wire rack

PICTURE PAGE 107

Serves 8

Preparation time: 1¼ hours

remaining grapefruit juice and set aside.

The cream: Whip until it forms a ribbon.

The grapefruit mixture: Put two-thirds of the *meringue italienne* in a bowl and set in a dish of crushed ice (see note below). Pour in the grapefruit juice mixture and mix lightly with a wire whisk. Stir in the whipped cream, a little at a time, then, using a spatula, carefully fold in the diced grapefruit taking care to separate the dice.

Assembling the moulds: Stand the moulds in a dish of crushed ice. Using one-third of the grapefruit mixture, divide it between the moulds. Using a soup spoon, spread the mixture up the sides of the moulds to line them.

Take 8 biscuit rounds and, using scissors, carefully cut out a small triangle and make 2 cuts from the opposite side, almost to the centre. Press one into each mould. Fill up the moulds with the remaining grapefruit mixture and top with a whole biscuit round. Flatten the surface with a palette knife and scrape off any excess mixture.

Wrap the moulds in clingfilm and leave to set in the fridge for 4 hours, or freeze for 2 hours before serving.

The strawberry glaze: Soak the 3 leaves of gelatine in very cold water for 15 minutes. Drain.

Rub the strawberries through a sieve into a saucepan, stir in the sugar and bring to the boil. Take the pan off the heat and stir in the well-drained gelatine. Skim the surface if necessary, then leave to cool until the glaze is half-set.

· TO SERVE ·

Dip the base of the moulds in very hot water for a few seconds. Hold the moulds over a wire rack and press one side with your fingers so that the *Palmerosa* slips towards the other side. It will then slide easily out of the mould. Place on the rack and, using a spoon, coat each *Palmerosa* with strawberry glaze.

Use a palette knife to transfer them to individual serving plates. Pour a ribbon of fruit *coulis* around each one and decorate each plate with 6 raspberries or substitute strawberries for the decorative raspberries if you prefer. Serve very cold.

· STORAGE ·

The *Palmerosas* will keep in a cold fridge for at least 48 hours, and can be frozen for up to a week. Refrigerate or freeze them in the mould and glaze just before serving.

As with all desserts containing *meringue italienne*, you must make the full quantity to obtain a successful mixture; discard the remaining one-third, or keep it for another use.

DELICE AU CASSIS
(Blackcurrant delight)

· INGREDIENTS ·

350 g/11 oz blackcurrants

150 ml / 6 fl oz Sorbet
syrup (see page 168),
divided into 3 equal
quantities

4 leaves of gelatine

12 g/2 tsp powdered
milk

¼ vanilla pod

3 egg yolks

25 g/1 oz sugar

1 round Sponge biscuit
(see recipe 2, page 53),
20 cm/8 in diameter,
sliced into a circle
5 mm/¼ in thick

200 ml/7 fl oz *Crème de
cassis*

1 quantity *Meringue
italienne* (see page 58)

400 ml/14 fl oz double
cream

Granulated sugar, to
decorate

Serves 8

Preparation time: 45
minutes

Cooking time: 10 minutes

· PREPARATION ·

The blackcurrant purée: Set aside 14 blackcurrants for the decoration. Purée the rest in the blender with 50 ml/2 oz syrup, then pass the purée through a conical strainer.

The blackcurrant custard: Soak 2 gelatine leaves in cold water for 15 minutes, then drain. Reserve 2 tbsp blackcurrant purée and put the rest in a saucepan. Add the powdered milk and vanilla and bring to the boil.

Combine the egg yolks and sugar in a bowl and whisk until they form a ribbon.

Pour the boiling blackcurrant purée onto the egg mixture, whisking continuously, then pour this custard back into the pan and set over low heat, stirring continuously with a spatula until the custard is thick enough to coat the spatula. Do not allow it to boil.

Take the pan off the heat and stir the drained gelatine into the custard. Discard the vanilla, then pass the custard through a conical strainer into a bowl and leave to cool, stirring occasionally to prevent a skin from forming.

The sponge: Place the sponge circle on the cake board. Mix together 50 ml/2 fl oz syrup and 1 tbsp of the reserved blackcurrant purée and brush this mixture over the sponge. Place the flan ring around the sponge.

The blackcurrant mousse: When the custard is lukewarm, gently fold in one-sixth of the *meringue italienne*, then the *crème de cassis*, using a balloon whisk. Beat the cream until it forms a ribbon and, with a wooden spatula, gently fold it into the mixture. You must now assemble the dessert immediately, before the gelatine causes the mousse to set.

Assembling the délice: Fill the flan ring with blackcurrant mousse and carefully smooth over the surface with a palette knife. Place in the freezer or a very cold fridge for several hours.

To glaze: Soak the 2 remaining gelatine leaves in cold water for 15 minutes, then drain well.

You can glaze the dessert with the flan ring in place, which will give you a neat, drip-free border, or remove the ring first if you prefer. To remove it, heat the outside of the ring over a gas flame for a few seconds, then slide the ring upwards, rotating it slightly.

Mix together the remaining syrup and blackcurrant purée and stir in the well-drained gelatine. Leave to cool, then use it to glaze the top of the dessert. Keep the *délice* in the flan ring and glaze just before serving.

· EQUIPMENT ·

Blender or food processor

1 saucepan

1 mixing bowl

1 × 24 cm/10 in round cake
board

1 flan ring, 22 cm/8½ in
diameter, 3.5 mm/1½ in deep

Conical strainer

PICTURE PAGE 110

· TO SERVE ·

If you have not already done so, remove the flan ring by sliding a knife blade dipped in hot water between the dessert and the ring. Roll the reserved blackcurrants in granulated sugar and decorate the top of the *délice*.

Serve the dessert whole, and slice it at the table with a knife dipped in hot water before cutting each slice.

· STORAGE ·

Unglazed and in the flan ring, the *délice* will keep in the fridge for several days, or for 2 weeks in the freezer.

· NOTES ·

Since it is difficult to divide the recipe for *meringue italienne*, you may prefer to prepare two of these *délices* at the same time and keep one for another occasion.

DELICE AUX FRUITS
DE LA PASSION
(Passion fruit delight)

· INGREDIENTS ·

9 passion fruit

450 ml/16 fl oz sieved passion fruit pulp (from about 45-50 fruits)

7 leaves of gelatine

100 ml/3½ fl oz milk

40 g/1½ oz powdered milk

½ vanilla pod, split

10 egg yolks

70 g/2½ oz sugar

1 round Sponge biscuit, 20 cm/8 in diameter (see recipe 2, page 53)

150 ml/5 fl oz Sorbet syrup (see page 168)

100 ml/3½ fl oz vodka

1 quantity *Meringue italienne* (see page 58)

675 ml/24 fl oz double cream

Juice of 1 orange, strained

· PREPARATION ·

The passion fruit: Cut a thin slice off both ends of 8 of the passion fruit, so that they will stand firmly, then cut them in half horizontally. Using a small spoon, scoop out about one-third of the pulp from each shell into a saucepan. Wrap the passion fruit shells in clingfilm and place in the fridge.

The passion fruit custard: Soak 6 of the gelatine leaves in very cold water for 20 minutes, then drain well.

In a saucepan, combine 350 ml/12 fl oz sieved passion fruit pulp, the milk, powdered milk and the split vanilla pod and bring to the boil. Put the egg yolks and sugar in a bowl and immediately whisk to a ribbon consistency.

Take the pan off the heat and pour the boiling milk mixture onto the yolks, stirring continuously. Set over low heat and cook, stirring continuously with a spatula, until the custard is thick enough to coat the spatula; do not let the custard boil. Take the pan off the heat and stir in the well-drained gelatine.

Remove the vanilla pod, then, when the gelatine has dissolved completely, pass the custard through a conical strainer and leave to cool, stirring from time to time.

The sponge: Cut the sponge horizontally into 2 circles, each about 5 mm/¼ in thick. You will have about half the sponge left over. Place a sponge circle on each cake board and brush with a mixture of 50 ml/2 fl oz syrup, 100 ml/4 fl oz sieved

· EQUIPMENT ·

2 saucepans

2 bowls

1 conical strainer

2 × 24 cm/10 in round cake boards

2 flan rings, 22 cm/8½ in diameter, 3.5 cm/1½ in deep

PICTURE PAGE 111

Continued on page 134

DELICE AU CASSIS

1

1

Cut a slice 5 mm/¼ in thick from the sponge biscuit for the base and place on the cake board.

2

Brush with a mixture of syrup and blackcurrant purée for moistness and flavour.

2

3

Gently fold the meringue into the cooled blackcurrant custard, using a wire whisk.

4

With a wooden spatula, carefully fold the whipped cream into the mixture until well blended.

3

4

5

Immediately pour this mousse over the sponge base and fill up the flan ring. This must be done quickly before the mousse sets.

6

Smooth the surface of the mousse with a palette knife to make it completely level. Chill in the fridge or freezer for several hours.

5

6

7

To glaze: pour the cooled glaze over the top of the mousse, starting at the centre and spreading the glaze to the edges with a palette knife.

8

With the point of a knife, immediately prick out any air bubbles from the glaze. If the flan ring is still in place, slide a knife between it and the délice and slide off

7

8

LA TRUFFE:
SAUCE ANGLAISE AU CAFE
(Chocolate truffle cake with coffee custard)

· INGREDIENTS ·

1 x 20 cm/8 in Genoise
sponge (see page 60),
made with 160 g/5½ oz
flour and 80 g/3½ oz
cocoa powder

50 ml/2 fl oz Sorbet
syrup (see page 168)

2 tbsp Cognac

475 g/17 oz bitter
couverture or plain
chocolate

475 ml/17 fl oz double
cream

10 g/1 tsp cocoa powder,
to decorate

500 ml/18 fl oz
coffee-flavoured *Crème
anglaise* (see page 70)

Serves 8

*Preparation time: 25
minutes*

· EQUIPMENT ·

*1 flan ring, 22 cm/8½ in
diameter, 3.5 cm/1½ in deep*

*1 × 24 cm/10 in round cake
board*

1 bowl

Bain-marie

We were given this quick and easy recipe by a colleague, Jean Masson, who prepared it at a seminar of the *Maîtres Pâtissiers de France* some 10 years ago. Since then, it has proved one of our most popular desserts.

· PREPARATION ·

The chocolate sponge base: Slice a 5 mm/¼ in thick circle off the top of the sponge and keep the rest in the fridge or freezer to use another time. Place the circle on the cake board and brush with a mixture of syrup and Cognac.

Set the flan ring around the sponge.

The truffle mixture: Roughly chop the *couverture* or chocolate and put in a bain-marie. Melt the chocolate gently, without letting it reach more than 35°C/95°F.

Put the cream in a bowl and whip until it forms a light ribbon. Pour half the melted chocolate into the cream and mix well with a whisk, but do not overwork the mixture. Add the remaining chocolate and beat very lightly until the mixture is homogenous, but stop before it separates. Pour the mixture into the flan ring, and with a palette knife push it outwards from the centre towards the edges, taking care not to leave any little gaps. Smooth the surface with the palette knife.

Place in the fridge for at least 30 minutes, until the truffle mixture has set.

· TO SERVE ·

To remove the flan ring, heat the outside of the ring over a gas flame for a few seconds, or dip the blade of a fine knife into boiling water and run it between the inside of the ring and the dessert, then rotate the circle slightly and lift it off.

Sprinkle the top with cocoa and serve.

Some *crème anglaise*, flavoured to taste with instant coffee, makes a superb accompaniment to this dessert. Serve it separately in a sauceboat.

· STORAGE ·

This truffle cake will keep well, still in the flan ring, for 2 days in the fridge, or 2 weeks in the freezer.

HOT SWEETS AND DESSERTS

*I*n winter, more than in any other season, one longs for a hot pudding. Special favourites at this bleak time of year include hot fruit fritters, plain or souffléd *crêpes* flavoured with vanilla, orange blossom water or Grand Marnier and *gratins* of fresh fruits.

Everyone is impressed by a soufflé, which testifies to a great deal of time and effort on the part of the hostess. Actually, the soufflé base (called *l'appareil*) can be prepared well in advance of the meal and kept at room temperature. Then, at the last moment, you need only beat the egg whites, fold them in to the *appareil*, pour the mixture into the soufflé dishes and cook at once.

CREPES DANIEL PINAUDIER

· INGREDIENTS ·

250 g/9 oz flour
30 g/1 oz sugar
Pinch of salt
4 eggs
650 ml/22 fl oz milk, boiled and cooled
200 ml/7 fl oz double cream
Flavouring of your choice
30 g/1 oz clarified butter

Serves 10

Preparation time: 10 minutes, plus at least 1 hour resting time

Cooking time: 1–2 minutes for each crêpe

· PREPARATION ·

Combine the flour, sugar and salt in a bowl and add the eggs, 2 at a time, mixing well with a spatula. Stir in one-third of the milk until you have a smooth, homogenous batter. Pour in the cream and the rest of the milk and leave to rest in a cool place for at least an hour before cooking the *crêpes*.

· TO COOK ·

Stir the batter and add your chosen flavouring.

Brush the frying pans or *crêpe* pan with clarified butter and heat them. Ladle in a little batter and cook for 1 or 2 minutes on each side, turning the *crêpe* with a palette knife or tossing it.

· TO SERVE ·

Roll or fold the *crêpes* into half or four and eat them as soon as they are cooked. Choose your own favourite flavouring — vanilla, orange blossom water, lemon zest or Grand Marnier, for example, or serve the *crêpes* plain; they are delicious sprinkled with sugar or served with jam or apple jelly (see page 70).

· EQUIPMENT ·

1 bowl
1 or 2 round frying pans, 30 cm/12 in diameter or a crêpe pan, 12 cm/5 in diameter

C H R I S T M A S   P U D D I N G

· INGREDIENTS ·

550 g/18 oz raisins
375 g/13 oz sultanas
375 g/13 oz currants
200 g/7 oz chopped almonds
400 g/14 oz finely grated suet
Zest and juice of 1 orange
Zest and juice of 1 lemon
1 apple, unpeeled, cored and grated
1 carrot, peeled and grated
250 g/9 oz fresh white breadcrumbs or brioche crumbs
250 g/9 oz flour
400 g/14 oz raw Demerara sugar
6 eggs
½ tsp salt
½ tsp ground cinnamon
1 heaped tsp ground mixed spice
110 g/4 oz candied mixed peel, finely chopped
110 g/4 oz glacé cherries, finely diced
1 glass brandy, plus 160 ml/5 fl oz for after the puddings are cooked
1 bottle (340 ml/12 fl oz) of Guinness or stout
150 g/5 oz clarified butter, for greasing
BRANDY SAUCE (for 10 people):
500 ml/18 fl oz double cream
70 g/2½ oz sugar
8 g/1 tsp potato flour, mixed with 1 tbsp milk
70 ml/3 fl oz brandy

Christmas pudding is divine, particularly this recipe, which Albert was given more than 30 years ago by Mrs. Bradbrook, a superb English cook. At the beginning of every year, we make our Christmas pudding for family and friends to enjoy the following Christmas; they also make a wonderful present. And we keep a few from previous years so that we can enjoy the indescribably glorious taste of a 3- or 4-year-old Christmas pudding.

· PREPARATION ·

Combine all the ingredients in a mixing bowl, except 160 ml/5 fl oz brandy and the clarified butter. Mix well.

Press a piece of greaseproof paper firmly over the mixture and place in the fridge for 48 hours.

Moulding the puddings: Preheat the oven to 150°C/ 300°F/gas 2.

Stir the pudding mix once more with a spatula, then divide the mixture between the 4 basins. Press down firmly with a spoon so that the puddings are very compact. Wipe the inside rim and the outsides of the basins with a damp cloth.

Cut out four 18 cm/7 in circles of greaseproof paper and brush with a little clarified butter. Place the circles over the puddings and press down firmly so that the paper sticks and makes a steamproof seal.

· TO COOK ·

Lay a circle of slightly dampened muslin over each basin, stretch tautly and tie the muslin tightly with string under the rim.

Place the puddings in a roasting pan lined with greaseproof paper and pour in enough boiling water to come halfway up the sides of the basins. Cover the pan with foil and cut a hole about 5 cm/2 in wide in the centre, making sure that it is not immediately above a pudding.

Cook in the preheated oven for 8 hours, checking the water level every 2 hours; it should always come halfway up the sides of the basins. Top up with boiling water when necessary.

· TO COOL ·

Take the puddings out of the roasting pan and put in a cool place for 24 hours.

· STORAGE ·

Remove the butter muslin, wash it and leave to dry. Leave the

· EQUIPMENT ·

1 large mixing bowl
4 × 850 ml/1½ pt china pudding basins, which must be scrupulously clean
Greaseproof paper
4 circles of butter muslin, 28 cm/11 in diameter
Kitchen string
1 roasting pan, at least 8 cm/3¼ in deep
Aluminium foil
1 saucepan
1 pressure cooker or steamer

Continued on page 146

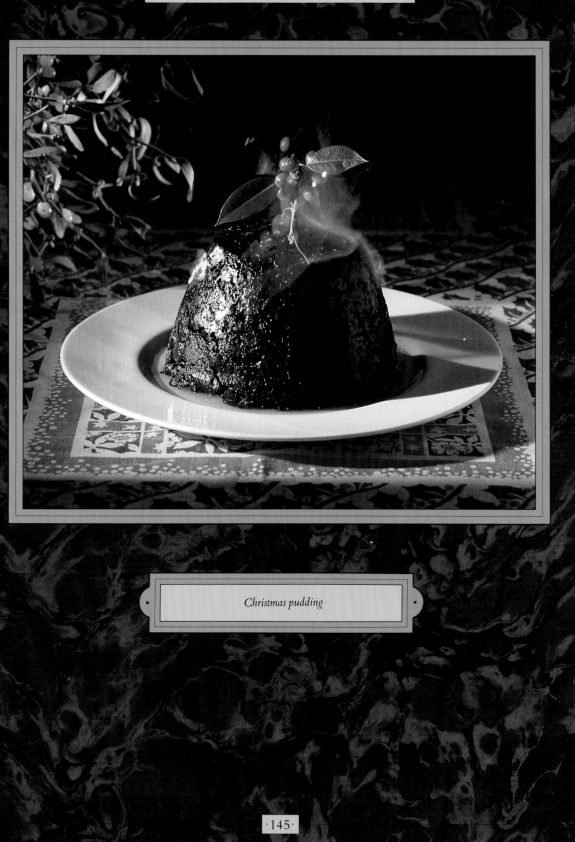

Christmas pudding

Makes 4 puddings, each
serving 10

Preparation time: 2 hours, to
be done 1-5 years in advance

Cooking time: 8 hours, plus
2½ hours heating

greaseproof paper in place. Carefully clean the inside rims and outsides of the basins.

Lift up one edge of the greaseproof paper and sprinkle each pudding with one-quarter of the brandy, then replace the paper to make an airtight seal.

Stretch the washed muslin over the basins and tie tightly with string. Brush with clarified butter to make them more or less watertight. Keep in the fridge until next Christmas, or even longer. . .

· THE BRANDY SAUCE ·

Put the cream and sugar in a saucepan, bring to the boil, then lower the heat and reduce gently by a quarter. Stir in the potato flour and boil for 1 minute. Add the brandy.

Keep the sauce hot without letting it boil.

· TO HEAT THE PUDDING ·

Place the pudding in a pressure cooker without the valve, or in a steamer and steam for 2½ hours.

· TO SERVE ·

Remove the cloth and greaseproof paper and unmould the pudding into a shallow dish. Decorate the top with a sprig of holly and bring the pudding to the table. If you like, flame with a little warmed brandy before serving. Serve the brandy sauce separately in a sauceboat, or serve the pudding with brandy butter made with creamed, softened butter, sifted icing sugar and brandy to taste.

FEUILLETES TIEDES AUX
RAISINS, SABAYON AU KIRSCH
(Warm feuilletés with grapes and Kirsch-flavoured sabayon)

· PREPARATION ·

Preheat the oven to 220°C/425°F/gas 8.

The grapes: Peel them and scoop out the pips with a small spoon, leaving the grapes whole and taking care not to spoil the shape. Place in a bowl and sprinkle over a little Kirsch. Set aside.

The feuilletés: On a lightly floured surface, roll out the pastry to a thickness of about 5 mm/¼ in. Using the larger pastry cutter, cut out 4 circles and place on a baking sheet lightly brushed with cold water. Leave to rest in the fridge for at least 30 minutes before baking. Glaze the tops of the pastry circles

· INGREDIENTS ·

400 g/14 oz white grapes
150 ml/5 fl oz Kirsch
Pinch of flour
350 g/12 oz Puff pastry (see pages 42-3)
Eggwash, made with 1 tbsp milk and 1 egg yolk
40 g/1½ oz icing sugar
120 g/4 oz sugar
100 ml/4 fl oz water
6 egg yolks
4 small sprigs of mint

Serves 4
Preparation time: 40 minutes
Cooking time: 12 minutes

with eggwash, then press down the smaller pastry cutter onto the pastry to mark out a lid. Use the point of a knife to mark criss-crosses on the lids.

· TO COOK ·

Bake the *feuilletés* in the preheated oven for 10 minutes, then remove from the oven, sprinkle with icing sugar and return to the oven for a further 2 minutes to give them a beautiful glaze. Transfer to a wire rack.

Run the point of a knife round the marked edge of the lids and lift off. Keep the baked pastry cases and lids warm.

The sabayon: Combine the sugar and water in a small saucepan, bring to the boil, then leave to cool.

Add the egg yolks and 100 ml/4 fl oz Kirsch, set over low heat and whisk continuously until you have a smooth, rich mousse. Increase the heat and continue to whisk until the sauce has a ribbon consistency. Stir in the remaining Kirsch and take the pan off the heat.

· TO SERVE ·

Gently warm the grapes. Place the *feuilletés* on individual plates and put a spoonful of *sabayon* in each. Drain the grapes well, then divide most of them between the *feuilletés*, reserving a few for the garnish. Fill the *feuilletés* with another spoonful of *sabayon* and pour the rest in a ribbon around each *feuilleté*. Prop the lids at an angle against the *feuilletés*, with one side on the edge of the plate. Garnish the *sabayon* with the reserved grapes and a sprig of mint.

· NOTES ·

To keep the pastry crisp and light, do not fill the *feuilletés* until just before serving. Make the *sabayon* at the last moment and use it immediately, or the lightness will be spoilt.

· EQUIPMENT ·

1 bowl
1 plain round pastry cutter, 9 cm/3½ in diameter
1 plain round pastry cutter, 7 cm/2¾ in diameter
1 baking sheet
Wooden or marble pastry board
1 small saucepan

PICTURE PAGE 149

ABOVE *Les gaufres (page 166)*
TOP RIGHT *Pêche rôtie au caramel noisetine*
(page 162)
BOTTOM RIGHT *Feuilleté tiède aux raisins, sabayon au*
Kirsch (page 146)

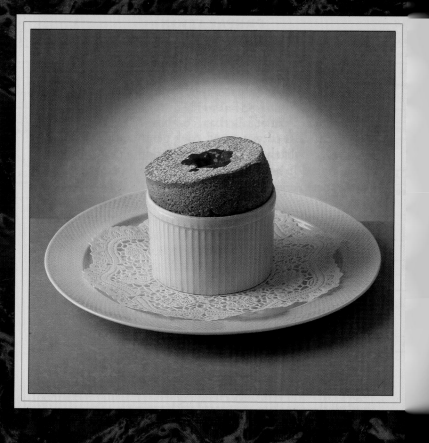

ABOVE *Soufflé chaud aux framboises (page 150)*
TOP RIGHT *Soufflé tiède aux poires, sauce chocolat (page 151)*
BOTTOM RIGHT *Soufflé tiède aux pêches (page 158)*

each soufflé with a pear fan and a mint sprig.

If you prefer, use 3 larger china soufflé dishes (10 cm/4 in diameter, 6 cm/2¼ in deep) and do not unmould the soufflés. Cook for 6 minutes, then arrange the diced pears and fans on top of the soufflés and serve the chocolate sauce separately in a sauceboat.

Serve immediately; this is a very delicate and fragile soufflé, which cannot be kept waiting.

SOUFFLES CHAUDS AUX MIRABELLES
(Hot mirabelle plum soufflés)

· INGREDIENTS ·

400 ml/14 fl oz milk
110 g/4 oz sugar, plus a pinch for the egg whites
50 g/2 oz flour
10 egg yolks
8 egg whites
550 g/1 lb 4 oz mirabelles in syrup, drained and syrup reserved
25 g/1 oz butter
100 ml/3½ fl oz mirabelle *eau de vie*
For the soufflé dishes:
30 g/1 oz melted butter
70 g/2½ oz sugar
Icing sugar, to serve

Serves 6
Preparation time: 30 minutes
Cooking time: 10 minutes

· EQUIPMENT ·

2 saucepans
1 fine sieve
Electric mixer
1 baking sheet
6 individual soufflé dishes, 10 cm/4 in diameter, 6 cm/2¼ in deep

Mainly grown in Alsace, mirabelles are small yellow plums with a very distinctive flavour. They are relatively unfamiliar in this country, but are regarded as a delicacy by plum lovers.

· PREPARATION ·

Crème pâtissière: Combine the milk and two-thirds of the sugar in a saucepan and bring to the boil.

Place 6 egg yolks and the remaining sugar in a bowl and work together with a wooden spoon for several minutes. Add the flour and beat until the mixture is very smooth. Pour in the boiling milk, whisking continuously.

Return the mixture to the pan, set over high heat and boil, stirring continuously, for 3 minutes.

Pour the custard into a bowl. Flake a little butter over the surface or dust lightly with icing sugar to prevent a skin from forming. Leave at room temperature.

The mirabelles: Place the reserved syrup from the mirabelles in a pan and boil vigorously until reduced by half. Lower the heat, add 450 g/1 lb mirabelles and cook gently for 10 minutes, then rub through a sieve; the purée should have a softish consistency. If it seems too liquid, reduce over medium heat, whisking continuously. Set aside at room temperature. Place the remaining mirabelles in a bowl, pour over half the *eau de vie* and leave to macerate.

The soufflé dishes: Using a pastry brush, coat the insides of the dishes with melted butter.

Pour the sugar into one dish and rotate it so that the whole surface is well coated with sugar. Pour the excess sugar into the next dish and repeat the process with each dish.

Place a baking sheet in the oven and preheat to 220°C/425°F/gas 8.

1
Gently fold one-third of the beaten egg white into the mirabelle mixture, then fold in thé rest with a spatula.

1

2

2
Fill the dishes one-third full with the soufflé mixture.

3
Divide the halved mirabelles between the dishes. Fill with the remaining soufflé mixture and smooth the surface. Run the point of the knife around the edge of the mixture to help the soufflés rise.

3

4
After baking on the preheated baking sheet, dust with icing sugar and serve at once.

4

The soufflé mixture: Whisk the mirabelle purée into the *crème pâtissière*, then the remaining egg yolks and *eau de vie*.

Beat the egg whites until frothy, add a pinch of sugar and beat until soft peaks form.

Using the whisk, quickly beat one-third of the egg whites into the mixture, then, with a spatula, gently fold in the rest of the egg whites.

Spoon the mixture into the soufflé dishes so that they are one-third full. Cut the alcohol-soaked mirabelles in half and divide them between the dishes.

Fill to the top with the remaining mixture and smooth over the surface with a palette knife. Run the point of a knife around the edge of the mixture; this will help the soufflés to rise. (You should always do this for any hot soufflé.)

· TO COOK ·

Arrange the soufflés on the preheated baking sheet and cook for 10 minutes.

Serve immediately, dusted with icing sugar..

· NOTES ·

There will be sufficient mixture left to make an extra soufflé, so you can be generous with your servings.

ABOVE *Crêpe soufflée à l'orange et au Grand Marnier (page 159)*
RIGHT *Pithiviers (page 160)*

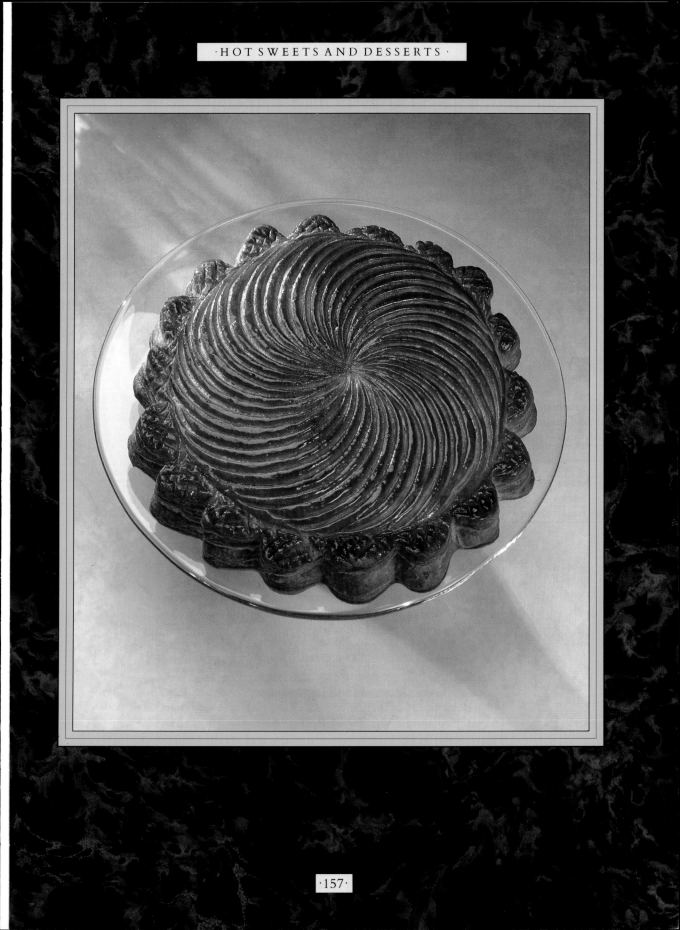

PITHIVIERS

· PREPARATION ·

The pastry: Cut the pastry into 2 parts, one weighing 350 g/
12 oz and the other 250 g/9 oz.

First make the base: on a lightly floured surface, roll out the
smaller piece of dough, turning it frequently by one-quarter
turn until you have a circle about 28 cm/11 in diameter and
2 mm/$\frac{1}{16}$ in thick. Roll it loosely onto the rolling pin, then

1

*Spoon the filling into the centre
of the pastry base and brush the
edges with eggwash.*

2

*Unroll the top over the base and
press the edges together.*

3

*After chilling, mark the pattern
and cut the overhanging edge into
a scallop shape.*

4

*Mark curved 'sunray' lines from
the centre to the edge of the cake.*

5

*Glazed and marked ready for
baking.*

6

*Bake, then sprinkle with icing
sugar and bake again.*

· INGREDIENTS ·
600 g/1 lb 5 oz Puff
pastry (see pages 42-3)
Pinch of flour
300 g/10 oz Almond
cream (see page 65)
60 g/2 oz *Crème
pâtissière* (see page 61)
(optional)
1 tbsp white rum
(optional)
1 egg yolk, lightly
beaten with 1 tbsp milk
30 g/1 oz icing sugar

Serves 8
Preparation time: 15
minutes, plus 30 minutes
resting time
Cooking time: 40 minutes

unroll onto a baking sheet lightly brushed with cold water.

Next make the top: roll out the larger piece of dough in exactly the same way and to a circle of the same diameter; it should be about 3 mm/⅛ in thick.

To assemble: Mix together the almond cream and the *crème pâtissière* and stir in the rum if you are using it. (It is not essential to add *crème pâtissière* to the almond cream for the filling, but it makes it beautifully moist.) Spoon the mixture into the centre of the pastry base, then spread it with a palette knife to within 3-4 cm/1½ in of the edge. Glaze the exposed edge with eggwash.

Place the second circle on top and press the edges of the 2 circles firmly together so that they are well sealed.

Chill in the fridge for 30 minutes.

Marking out the pattern: Press down a *Pithiviers* marker, or a flan ring or shallow plate 24 cm/9½ in diameter on top of the *Pithiviers*. With a small sharp knife, cut the overhanging dough into a scallop-shaped border. Remove the marker.

Glaze with eggwash, then, with the point of a knife, mark out faint lines from the centre of the cake to the edge, like sunrays, in the shape of a rosette. Mark the scalloped edges with diagonal lines.

· TO COOK ·

Preheat the oven to 240°C/475°F/gas 10. Bake the *Pithiviers* for 10 minutes, then lower the oven temperature to 200°C/400°F/gas 7 and cook for a further 25 minutes.

Increase the oven temperature to 220°C/425°F/gas 8. Sprinkle the *Pithiviers* with the icing sugar and bake for a final 5 minutes to give the cake a beautiful glaze.

· TO SERVE ·

Serve the *Pithiviers* warm with no further adornment; it will be wonderful. You can, if you wish, make a sauce to hand round separately in a sauceboat. Some apricot *coulis* or *crème anglaise* will enhance the flavour of the almond cream.

· STORAGE ·

To freeze the *Pithiviers*, assemble the cake, then freeze it unbaked, unglazed and unpatterned. To serve, remove from the freezer for 30 minutes, then glaze and mark the top. Bake while still frozen, allowing an extra 10 minutes cooking time.

It will keep in the freezer for up to a week.

· EQUIPMENT ·

Wooden or marble pastry
board
1 baking sheet
1 Pithiviers marker or flan
ring, 24 cm/9½ in diameter

PICTURE PAGE 157

EXOTIC FRUIT SORBETS

Presented in their shells: **1** *Prickly pear,*
2 *tamarillo or tree-tomato,* **3** *lime,* **4** *kumquat,*
5 *passion fruit,* **6** *rambutan,* **7** *pineapple, and*
8 *kiwi fruit (page 173).*

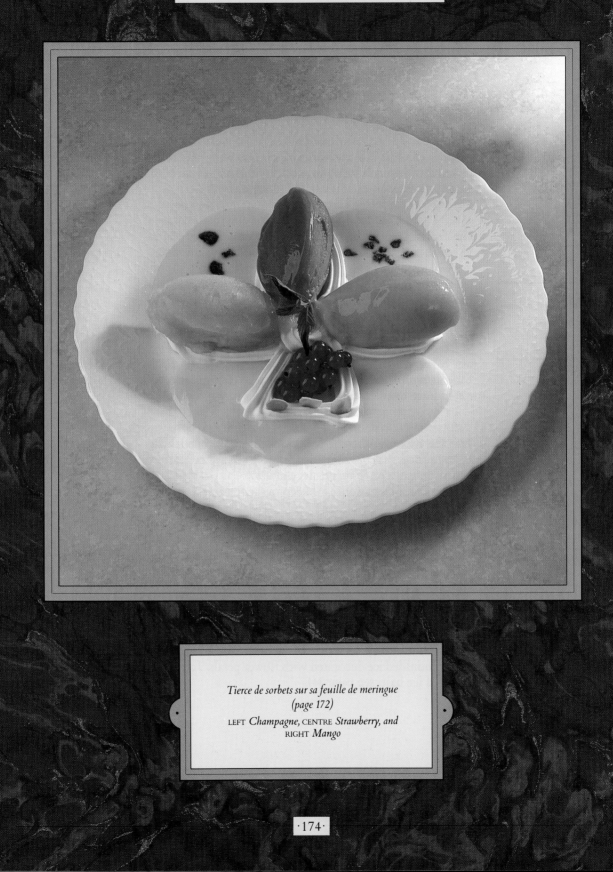

Tierce de sorbets sur sa feuille de meringue
(page 172)
LEFT *Champagne*, CENTRE *Strawberry, and*
RIGHT *Mango*

TOP LEFT *Sorbet à la tomate (page 169)*
TOP RIGHT *Glace amandine, sauce chocolat*
(page 177)
BOTTOM LEFT *Granité de poires au vin de*
Brouilly (page 185)
BOTTOM RIGHT *Petits vacherins glacés aux pistils*
de safran (page 186)

SORBET AU CHAMPAGNE OU SAUTERNES
(Champagne or Sauternes sorbet)

· INGREDIENTS ·
½ egg white

300 ml/11 fl oz Sorbet syrup (see page 168)

750 ml /1 bottle dry champagne, preferably pink

Juice of ½ lemon

Serves 6

Preparation time: 10 minutes

Churning time: 10-20 minutes

· PREPARATION ·

Beat the egg white very lightly with a fork.

Put the syrup in a bowl, pour over the champagne and stir with a spatula. Add the lemon juice, then the egg white and mix well.

Churn the mixture in the ice cream maker; depending on the model, it will take between 10 and 20 minutes. The sorbet should be smooth but very light.

· TO SERVE ·

Serve the sorbet in well-chilled glass dishes and decorate with wild strawberries in season.

· NOTES ·

Use pink champagne if possible as, once churned, it has a lovely, more delicate colour than white champagne.

The sorbet should be eaten as soon as it is churned to preserve its smoothness and light texture. It may be served as a dessert or in the middle of a meal.

You can use 750 ml/1 bottle Sauternes instead of the champagne; use only 250 ml/9 fl oz syrup to a bottle of Sauternes. This sorbet makes a superb accompaniment to *foie gras*.

· EQUIPMENT ·
1 bowl

Ice cream maker

GLACE AU MIEL
(Honey ice cream)

· INGREDIENTS ·
100 ml/4 fl oz double cream

FOR THE CREME ANGLAISE:

6 egg yolks

75 g/2½ oz sugar

500 ml/18 fl oz milk

150 g/5 oz honey

· PREPARATION ·

The custard: Boil the milk with the honey, then make a *creme anglaise* following the method on page 70. Use only 75 g/2½ oz sugar, as the honey is very sweet.

· CHURNING ·

When the custard is cold, pass it through a conical strainer into the ice cream maker and churn for about 10 minutes, so that the ice cream is still fairly soft. Add the cream and churn for a further 20 minutes, depending on the machine, until the ice cream is firm.

Serve at once or keep in the freezer until needed — but only for a short time.

· EQUIPMENT ·
Ice cream maker

Conical strainer

Serves 6

Preparation time: 15 minutes

Cooking time: about 8 minutes

Churning time: about 30 minutes

· TO SERVE ·

Everyone will enjoy this honey ice cream. To serve it in a really original way, put a spoonful of ice cream into a chilled coffee cup and pour over some very hot coffee. Do this at the table so that your guests can immediately taste and enjoy this delectable contrast of the very hot and the very cold.

GLACE AMANDINE, SAUCE CHOCOLAT
(Hazelnut praline ice cream)

· INGREDIENTS ·

60 g/2 oz whole hazelnuts

60 g/2 oz sugar

1 tsp peanut oil

1 tsp instant coffee powder

½ quantity *Crème anglaise*, made without vanilla (see page 70)

50 ml/2 fl oz double cream

CHOCOLATE SAUCE

150 g/5 oz bitter chocolate *or* plain *couverture*

150 ml/6 fl oz double cream

25 g/1 oz butter

Serves 4

Preparation time: 15 minutes

Churning time: 10-20 minutes

· PREPARATION ·

Preheat the oven to 240°C/475°F/gas 10.

The hazelnuts: Spread the nuts on a baking tray and place in the preheated oven or under the grill for 5 minutes, until the skin blisters and the hazelnuts turn golden brown. Rub with a cloth to remove the skins and keep the nuts in a warm place.

Caramelizing the nuts: Put the sugar in a heavy-based pan and heat, without any added liquid, stirring continuously, until it has dissolved completely and is a lovely pale gold. Throw in the hazelnuts and cook for 1 minute. Pour the mixture onto a lightly oiled baking sheet and leave to cool at room temperature for about 20 minutes. When the praline is completely cold, crush with a rolling pin and keep at room temperature.

To churn: Combine the coffee powder and the cold *crème anglaise* in a bowl and whisk together. Stir in the double cream and pour the mixture into the ice cream maker.

Depending on the model, it will take between 10 and 20 minutes. When the ice cream is ready, stir in the cold praline. Serve immediately or keep in the freezer.

The chocolate sauce: Make the sauce according to the recipe on page 67, allowing about 50 ml/2 fl oz per person. Serve the hot sauce separately in a sauceboat.

· NOTES ·

Ice creams should be eaten as soon as they are churned; their texture and flavour will be much better. Never keep them in the freezer for more than a few hours.

· EQUIPMENT ·

1 baking sheet

1 sugar pan or saucepan

Ice cream maker

PICTURE PAGE 175

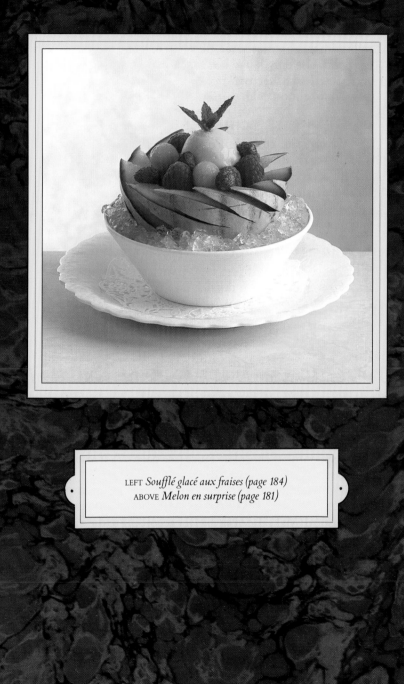

LEFT *Soufflé glacé aux fraises (page 184)*
ABOVE *Melon en surprise (page 181)*

LEFT, TOP TO BOTTOM *Petit toast au fromage blanc et aux câpres, Petit choux au fromage, Petit toast aux oeufs durs et cerfeuil, Croustade d'oeuf de caille, sauce cocktail.*
FAR RIGHT *Blini au caviar* and RIGHT *Blini au caviar (salmon roe).* TOP RIGHT *Petite bouchée au fenouil (pages 190–3)*

MAIN PICTURE, TOP TIER *Noisettes caramelisées au chocolat;* CENTRE TIER *Tuiles dentelles à l'orange;* BOTTOM TIER *(clockwise) Allumettes glacées, Madeleines au miel, Truffes au chocolat, Macarons and Palmiers. (See pages 194–204)* OPPOSITE, TOP TO BOTTOM *Palmier, Truffe au chocolat, Allumette glacée, Tuile dentelle à l'orange.* BELOW LEFT *Noisette caramelisée au chocolat,* and BELOW *Madeleine au miel.*

MACARONS
(Macaroons)

· INGREDIENTS ·

225 g/8 oz icing sugar

125 g/4 oz ground almonds

4 egg whites

25 g/1 oz sugar

Flavourings:

½ tsp vanilla essence, *or*

½ tsp raspberry essence, plus a few drops red food colouring (optional) *or* 20 g/¾ oz sifted cocoa powder

Makes about 36

Preparation time: 15 minutes

Cooking time: 10 minutes

These are some of the most delicate petits fours, both to make and to eat. They should be shiny and smooth and, above all, very moist in the centre.

· PREPARATION ·

The icing sugar and ground almonds: Sift the icing sugar, then sift again with the ground almonds and the cocoa powder, if you are making chocolate macaroons. Keep the mixture on a sheet of greaseproof paper.

The egg whites: Beat until half-risen, then add the sugar and beat until stiff. Add the chosen flavouring, then increase the speed to high and beat for 1 minute, until very firm.

The macaroon mixture: Sprinkle the icing sugar and almond mixture over the egg whites and fold in gently with a spatula. Mix together until they are thoroughly blended and the mixture is very smooth.

Piping the macaroons: Pipe out the mixture into small, even rounds, about 2 cm/¾ in diameter onto a baking sheet lined with greaseproof paper. Pipe the macaroons in staggered rows, about 2.5 cm/1 in apart.

· TO COOK ·

Method 1: Preheat the oven to 180°C/350°F/gas 4. Leave the macaroons at room temperature for about 15 minutes, until a light crust forms, then bake for 10 minutes, leaving the oven door slightly ajar (about 2.5 cm/1 in) to allow the steam to escape from the oven.

Method 2: Preheat the oven to 220-230°C/425-450°F/gas 7-8. After piping, bake the macaroons immediately in the preheated oven for 2 or 3 minutes, then quickly transfer them to another oven heated to 180°C/350°F/gas 4 and bake for a

· EQUIPMENT ·

Electric mixer

Piping bag and plain 1 cm/½ in nozzle

4 baking sheets

Greaseproof paper

Wire rack

PICTURE PAGES 202-3

1

Fill the piping bag with the prepared macaroon mixture.

2

Pipe a little mixture under the paper to stop it from moving on the baking sheet. Pipe out the mixture in staggered rows, spacing the macaroons 2.5 cm/1 in apart.

2

3

When the macaroons are cooked, pour a little cold water between the greaseproof paper and the baking sheet.

3

4

4

After 2 or 3 minutes, lift the macaroons off the paper and press the underside with your fingers to make a small indentation.

5

Spread the underside of the macaroons with redcurrant jelly or the filling of your choice.

6

Sandwich the macaroons together in pairs and leave to cool on a wire rack.

5

6

further 6 minutes, leaving the oven door slightly ajar.

Whichever method you use, place an empty baking sheet under the sheet containing the macaroons to protect the bottoms and prevent them from burning. As soon as the macaroons are cooked, run a little cold water between the greaseproof paper and the baking sheet which will detach the macaroons. After 2 or 3 minutes, lift off the macaroons with your fingers and gently stick them together in pairs.

If you like, you can use a palette knife to smear on a little redcurrant jelly, chocolate *ganache* etc. before sticking them together.

Leave to cool on a wire rack.

· STORAGE ·

Packed in an airtight container, the macaroons will freeze very well.

TEA AND PICNIC CAKES

*In the hamper are Cake au citron (page 211) and
Cake marbré (page 210). On the hamper are
Cake aux fruits confits (page 209) and Cake au
vin de fruits (page 212).*

CHAPTER
· 5 ·

TEA AND
PICNIC CAKES

*T*hese cakes, which can all be made well in advance, are ideal for afternoon tea and, because they are easily transportable, perfect for picnics. Serve them with a red fruit *coulis*, fruit compote or jam, or with chilled fresh fruits; this will enhance the flavour and make the cakes even more appetizing.

Our own favourite is the delicately scented lemon cake, the recipe for which was given to us by our friend and colleague from Paris, Denis Ruffel.

CAKE AUX FRUITS CONFITS
(Fruit cake)

· INGREDIENTS ·

125 g/4 oz butter, plus
30 g/1 oz for greasing
125 g/4 oz sugar
1 × 70 g/size 1 egg, at room temperature (20°C/68°F)
1 egg yolk
125 g/4 oz moist candied fruits, diced
60 g/2 oz raisins
Few drops vanilla essence, lemon juice or orange blossom water
5 g/2 tsp baking powder
150 g/5 oz flour
1 tbsp full-flavoured rum
50 g/2 oz apricot jam, sieved
30 g/1 oz flaked almonds or 6 glacé cherries, halved

Serves 6
Preparation time: 25 minutes, plus 20 minutes chilling
Cooking time: 40 minutes

· PREPARATION ·

Preheat the oven to 240°C/475°F/gas 10.

In a bowl, cream together the butter and sugar until soft. Beat in the warmed whole egg, then the yolk. If the mixture separates, stand the bowl in a bain-marie for a few seconds, beating all the time. Using a spatula, stir in the candied fruits, raisins and the flavouring of your choice.

Sift together the flour and baking powder. Fold into the mixture, using a spatula. Cover the bowl with clingfilm or a plate and leave in the fridge for 20 minutes.

· TO COOK ·

Brush the inside of the loaf tin with butter and line it with the paper which should come 2-3 cm/about 1 in above the top of the tin. Pour the cake mixture into the tin, taking care not to drop any onto the paper.

Bake in the preheated oven for 7 minutes, then lower the temperature to 180°C/350°F/gas 5 and cook for a further 33 minutes. To check when the cake is ready, insert a skewer or the point of a very fine knife into the centre; it should come out clean.

· TO DECORATE ·

As soon as the cake comes out of the oven, sprinkle over the rum. Leave the cake in the tin for 10-15 minutes, then unmould it onto a wire rack.

Cut the paper into zigzags all round the cake, leaving the paper slightly higher than the top of the cake.

Brush the top with warmed apricot jam and decorate with the almonds or halved glacé cherries.

· TO SERVE ·

It is always best to serve a cake at least 12 hours after it has been baked and always at room temperature. Serve it thinly sliced, on its own or with a *crème anglaise* or some home-made jam.

· STORAGE ·

You can freeze this cake for up to a week. Sprinkle over the rum, but do not coat with the apricot jam. Leave the cake to cool slightly, then wrap it in clingfilm while still tepid and freeze.

Twenty-four hours before you want to eat it, place the cake in the fridge for 12 hours, then leave at room temperature for 12 hours before coating and decorating.

· EQUIPMENT ·

1 bowl
1 loaf tin, 23 × 9 cm/9 × 3½ in, 7 cm/2¼ in deep, 19 × 6.5 cm/7½ × 2½ in at the base
Thick white or greaseproof paper
Wire rack

PICTURE PAGES 206-7

CAKE MARBRE
(Marble cake)

· INGREDIENTS ·

240 g/8 oz softened
butter, plus 30 g/1 oz for
greasing

300 g/10 oz icing sugar,
sifted

6 × 50 g/size 5 eggs, at
room temperature
(20°C/68°F)

280 g/10 oz flour

5 g/2 tsp baking powder

40 g/1½ oz cocoa
powder, sifted, or 40 g/
1½ oz plain chocolate,
melted

60 g/2 oz moist candied
orange peel, finely diced

Serves 10-12

Preparation time: 30
minutes, plus 20 minutes
chilling

Cooking time: 1 hour for the
large cake, 15 minutes for the
small cakes

This cake is similar to a classic pound cake. For a different flavour, replace the cocoa powder or melted chocolate with instant coffee powder. It is also nice to add some dried fruits, like stoned apricots or prunes. Add them to the unflavoured mixture.

· PREPARATION ·

Preheat the oven to 220°C/425°F/gas 8.

In a bowl, lightly whisk together the softened butter and icing sugar until pale. Do not overwork.

Separate the eggs and set aside the whites.

Add the yolks, one at a time, to the butter and sugar, stirring well to mix thoroughly.

Sift together the flour and baking powder, then fold into the mixture with a spatula. Stop mixing as soon as the mixture is homogenous.

Beat the egg whites until soft peaks form, then, using a spatula, fold them gently into the mixture.

Pour one-third of the mixture into a bowl. Stir in the cocoa powder or melted chocolate.

Stir the diced orange peel into the remaining mixture.

Cover the bowls with clingfilm or plates and refrigerate for about 20 minutes.

· TO COOK ·

Brush the inside of the tin and moulds with butter. Line the large tin (but not the small moulds) with the paper, which should come 2-3 cm/about 1 in above the top of the tin.

Spoon the 2 mixtures alternately into the moulds to show the 2 distinct colours, or drop them in rivulets to give a marbled effect. Take care not to drop any mixture onto the paper.

Bake in the preheated oven for 7 minutes, then reduce the temperature to 190°C/375°F/gas 6 and cook the small cakes for a further 8 minutes. (The large cake will need about 53 minutes.) To check when the cakes are ready, insert a skewer or the point of a very fine knife into the centre; it should come out clean.

· TO DECORATE ·

Remove from the oven and unmould immediately. Place on a wire rack. For the large cake, either cut the paper into zigzags all round the cake, leaving the paper slightly higher than the top of the cake, or simply remove it altogether.

· EQUIPMENT ·

2 mixing bowls

1 loaf tin, 22 × 9 cm/
8½ × 3½ in, 8 cm/3 in deep,
19 × 7 cm/7½ × 2¼ in at
the base

6 small brioche moulds,
8 cm/3¼ in at the top,
4 cm/1½ in at the base,
3 cm/1¼ in deep, or 6 fluted
tartlet tins

Thick white or greaseproof
paper

Wire rack

PICTURE PAGES 206-7

· TO SERVE ·

It is best to serve a cake at least 12 hours after it has been baked. Serve at room temperature, thinly sliced. Sprinkle the top with a little icing sugar if you like.

· STORAGE ·

To freeze the cake for up to a week, let it cool slightly, then wrap in clingfilm while still tepid and freeze.

A day before you want to serve it, place the cake in the fridge for 12 hours then leave at room temperature for a further 12 hours.

CAKE AU CITRON
(Lemon cake)

· INGREDIENTS ·

Zest of 1 large lemon, finely grated

2 × 70 g/size 1 eggs or 3 × 50 g/size 5 eggs, at room temperature (20°C/68°F)

Pinch of salt

175 g/6 oz sugar

75 ml/3 fl oz double cream

140 g/4½ oz flour

2.5 g/1 tsp baking powder

50 g/2 oz butter, melted and cooled

20 ml/1 fl oz full-flavoured rum, plus 1 tbsp

30 g/1 oz butter, for greasing

75 g/3 oz apricot jam, sieved

For the icing:

80 g/3 oz icing sugar, sifted

Juice of 1 lemon

Serves 6

Preparation time: 15 minutes

Cooking time: 40 minutes

This excellent recipe was given to us by our friend and fellow *pâtissier*, Denis Ruffel. It is so delicate and delicious that once you have tasted a slice, you will not be able to resist another, then a third. . .

· PREPARATION ·

Preheat the oven to 200°C/400°F/gas 7.

In a bowl, whisk together the lemon zest, eggs, salt and sugar. Do not overwork.

Stir in the cream, then sift together the flour and baking powder and fold in. Finally, add the cooled melted butter and 20 ml/1 fl oz rum.

· TO COOK ·

Brush the inside of the loaf tin with butter and line it with the paper, which should come 2–3 cm/about 1 in above the top of the tin.

Pour the mixture into the tin, taking care not to drop any onto the paper.

Bake in the preheated oven for 7 minutes, then lower the temperature to 180°C/350°F/gas 5 and cook for a further 33 minutes. To check when the cake is ready, insert a skewer or the point of a very fine knife into the centre; it should come out clean.

· TO ICE ·

Unmould the cake as soon as it comes out of the oven. Place it on a wire rack set over a shallow dish and remove the paper. Sprinkle over the remaining rum.

Increase the oven temperature to 250°C/500°F/gas 10.

When the cake is cold, brush the top and sides with

· EQUIPMENT ·

1 mixing bowl

1 loaf tin,
23 × 9 cm/9 × 3½ in,
7 cm/2¼ in deep,
19 × 6.5 cm/7½ × 2½ in at the base

Thick white or greaseproof paper

Wire rack

PICTURE PAGES 206-7

warmed apricot jam. In a bowl, make the icing with the lemon juice and icing sugar exactly as you would with water. Spread the icing over the cake; any excess will be caught in the dish.

Place immediately in the very hot oven for about 15 seconds to 'set' the icing.

· TO SERVE ·

Unlike most cakes, this lemon cake can be served on the day it is made, as soon as it has cooled, although it is equally good 2 or 3 days later.

Eat this light cake on its own, or served with a chocolate mousse or *Oeufs à la neige* (see page 105). Serve it very thinly sliced.

· STORAGE ·

The cake will freeze very well for up to a week; sprinkle it with the rum, but do not glaze with the jam. Wrap in clingfilm and freeze while still slightly warm.

One day before you want to eat it, place the cake in the fridge for 12 hours, then for 12 hours at room temperature before coating with jam and icing.

CAKE AU VIN DE FRUITS
(Cake with fruit wine)

· INGREDIENTS ·

30 g/1 oz butter, for greasing
2 eggs, at room temperature (20°C/68°F)
130 g/4 oz sugar
100 g/3½ oz moist mixed crystallized fruits, diced
80 g/3 oz raisins
80 g/3 oz sultanas
80 g/3 oz glacé cherries
450 ml/16 fl oz fruit wine (eg, plum or cherry)
340 g/11 oz flour
10 g/4 tsp baking powder

This cake contains no fats, which makes it perfect for people on a fat-free diet and makes it firmer and more compact than a classic cake — its texture is more like that of a malt loaf.

· PREPARATION ·

Preheat the oven to 240°C/475°F/gas 10.

In a bowl, whisk together the eggs and sugar until pale. With a spatula, fold in the diced crystallized fruits, the raisins, sultanas and cherries. Stir in the fruit wine.

Sift together the flour and baking powder, then, with a spatula, fold them into the cake mixture. As soon as they are thoroughly blended, stop mixing. Do not overwork the mixture. Cover the bowl with clingfilm or a plate and refrigerate for about 20 minutes.

· TO COOK ·

Brush the insides of the tin and moulds with butter. Line the large tin (but not the small moulds) with white or greaseproof paper, which should come 2-3cm/about 1 in above the top of the tin.

Pour two-thirds of the cake mixture into the large tin,

· EQUIPMENT ·

1 mixing bowl
1 loaf tin, 23 × 9 cm/ 9 × 3½in, 7 cm/2¾ in deep, 19 × 6.5 cm/7½ × 2½ in at the base
6 small brioche moulds, 8 cm/3¼ in at the top, 4 cm/1½ in at the base, 3 cm/1¼ in deep
Thick white or greaseproof paper
Wire rack

PICTURE PAGES 206-7

Serves 12

Preparation time: 15 minutes, plus 20 minutes chilling

Cooking time: 1 hour for the large cake, 15 minutes for the small cakes

taking care not to drop any onto the paper, and divide the rest between the small moulds.

Bake in the preheated oven for 7 minutes, then lower the temperature to 180°C/350°F/gas 5 and cook the small cakes for a further 8 minutes. (The large cake will need about 53 minutes.) To check when the cakes are ready, insert a skewer or the point of a very fine knife into the centre; it should come out clean.

· TO DECORATE ·

Leave the cakes in the moulds for 10–15 minutes, then unmould onto a wire rack.

For the large cake, either cut the paper into zigzags all round the cake, leaving the paper slightly higher than the top of the cake, or simply remove it altogether.

· TO SERVE ·

It is best not to serve a cake for at least 12 hours after it has been baked. Serve it at room temperature, thinly sliced, on its own or with fresh unsalted farm butter, if available.

· STORAGE ·

It will freeze well for up to a week. Leave to cool slightly, then wrap it in clingfilm while still tepid and freeze.

A full day before you want to eat it, place the cake in the fridge for 12 hours, then leave at room temperature for a further 12 hours.

CHAPTER
· 6 ·

DECORATION
AND
PRESENTATION

This chapter is intended to inspire everyone to try his hand at creating different decorations. Whichever method you use — piping, painting with food colouring or cocoa, *pastillage* or almond paste, or working with sugar in various forms — poured, blown, pulled, spun etc — it only requires a little application to produce an impressive result which will amaze those new to the art.

COOKING AND WORKING WITH SUGAR

*E*ven an amateur with no previous experience can be creative with sugar: just follow our methods and the recipes in this chapter and you will find it less difficult than you feared. Remember that when we took our first steps in this direction we were just sixteen years old.

By following all these rules, even total beginners can launch themselves into the art of working with sugar. Start by working with poured or pulled sugar before embarking on blown sugar, which is always more complex. If you want to create a big, important piece in blown sugar, it is better for two people to work together — one to blow and the other to fashion the decorative piece.

Beginners should space out their sugar-working sessions. Once or twice a week is quite enough; the skin on your hands must become accustomed to the heat, which can cause blisters, particularly on the fingertips.

· COOKING ·

It takes only a few simple gestures to weigh the sugar, moisten it with water and add cream of tartar or glucose. The pan, all clad in copper, set over direct heat, gentle at first, then fierce, is now entrusted with this boiling, seething mass until it becomes 'hard crack'. And while it cooks, your nimble fingertips, dipped into icy water, will guard against the formation of crystals on the inside of the pan.

· COOLING ·

As the sugar is gently poured onto a lightly oiled marble, the outer edges will spread; fold them back inwards with a palette knife or metal scraper four or five times. By now, you can risk it with your fingertips.

· CONTACT ·

At last you can hold the sugar with your fingers — but not for long, because it is still extremely hot. As it makes contact with the marble, keep stretching the sugar and folding it back on itself; it will still feel very hot, but not unbearable. Now your fingers can hold the mass without making contact with the marble. After two or three minutes, hand and sugar are finally and completely united; they seem to have attained precisely the same temperature. The sugar bends, takes on a satin sheen. Suddenly it sings, it makes a slight cracking sound, it talks to you. Proud, beautiful, docile, it is now ready to be shaped into flowers, leaves, animals, what you will. This is the *pâtissier-confiseur's* highest form of artistic expression.

WORKING WITH SUGAR

It is absolutely vital to study closely the following rules and advice before embarking on our recipes.

· IMPORTANT RULES ·

• You should never attempt to cook sugar in a damp atmosphere (ie, when the humidity is high). The sugar will 'sweat' when you try to work it and, once pulled, it will lose its glossy brilliance.

• You must never work in a draught. Sugar loves heat and dryness and if subjected to a draught will be unmalleable and difficult to mould.

• Scrupulous cleanliness — both personal and material — is essential. All equipment and working areas must be spotless. The sugar pan should be washed with coarse salt and vinegar, then rinsed with fresh water and drained but not dried. Your marble slab, utensils, hands and nails must be immaculately clean.

Assuming that you have abided by these three cardinal rules, there are certain other important factors governing your choice of equipment and ingredients.

· EQUIPMENT ·

• Choose a pan made of untinned copper, which conducts heat rapidly and holds it well.

• Never use a wooden spatula; it may look clean, but wood absorbs flavours and grease and could ruin the sugar; the only exception is for *sucre rocher*.

• Always pour the water into the pan before the sugar, so that it dissolves more easily. Stir with a skimmer until the sugar has dissolved completely, then stop just before it begins to cook.

· INGREDIENTS ·

• The amount of glucose you add to the sugar and water will vary depending on the effect you wish to achieve. You can add 10-20 per cent more glucose to *sucre soufflé*, which will become more malleable; raise the cooking temperature by 1° or 2°C (about 25°F).

• A sugar thermometer graduating from 70°C/158°F to 200°C/392°F is indispensable for the amateur. Once you are practised in the art, you can gauge the exact stage the sugar has reached simply by looking and testing with your fingers (see table opposite). Plunge them into iced water, then into the sugar, then back into the water; you will not need a thermometer.

• The precise cooking temperature varies according to the weight of sugar being cooked. Where our recipes are for 1 kg (2 lb 2 oz) of sugar, you may prefer to prepare only half that quantity; reduce the temperature by 1° or 2° C (about 25°F). If you are doubling the quantities, increase the temperature by 1° or 2°C.

· TECHNIQUE ·

• As soon as the sugar begins to boil, cover the pan with a lid with a small hole in it; this will enable you to keep the thermometer vertical and will prevent it from burning on the sides of the pan. It will also be easier to read the temperature, since there will be less steam and condensation; alternatively, partially cover the pan with a lid. This will become saturated with condensation and droplets of water will drip down the sides of the pan into the sugar. This process is very important; it not only cleans the pan, but also prevents the sugar from solidifying.

• It is important when cooking sugar that the flame does not lick up the sides of the pan, or the sugar, which cooks faster at the edge, will become yellowish in colour.

If you want to colour the sugar, it is advisable to use powdered food colourings. The colours are brighter and more vibrant than liquid colourings.

Before using, dilute them in a few drops of 90° proof alcohol or Cognac or Armagnac. Add the colourings to the boiling sugar when it reaches 140°C/284°F. If you prefer, you can add the colouring to the sugar as soon as you pour it onto the marble slab. Pour a very few drops into the centre of the sugar mass.

It is very important to note, however, that colour must always be added to *sucre coulé* while it is cooking. Remember that it should be as transparent as glass, so be careful not to overdo the colouring. Pastel colours look much more attractive.

• Once sugar has reached the desired temperature, you must on no account take the thermometer out of the boiling liquid and plunge it into iced water. The sudden drop in temperature (from about 150°C/302°F to freezing) will play havoc with the temperature gauge, even if it doesn't actually break it.

• As soon as the sugar on the marble becomes satiny, it should be transferred to a special, very thick and heat-resistant plastic sheet.

• So that the sugar retains its heat and remains pliable, place it under an infra-red or radiant heat lamp. If you don't possess one, roll the sugar into a ball and place it on a sieve or baking sheet. Heat the oven to 100°-120°C/212°-248°F and work the sugar at the opening of the oven, with the door half-open.

• For a perfect result when working with *sucre coulé*, use a small gas jet to eliminate any air bubbles while you pour the sugar.

• Once you have made your sugar ornaments, place them in an airtight container which you have carefully prepared beforehand. Line the bottom with a dehydrating compound, such as silica gel, carbide or quicklime, covered with aluminium foil. Seal the container tightly and put in a dry place; your sugar decorations will keep for several weeks before you use them. This allows you to create really imposing competition pieces, which may have taken several months to prepare — or simply to make smaller decorations for a family celebration.

TEMPERATURES FOR SUGAR BOILING

°C	°F	Sugar stage	Method of testing
100	212	small gloss or thread	Take a little sugar syrup between your thumb and index finger and stretch them apart. Short threads will form.
104	219	large gloss or thread	Test as above; longer, stronger threads will form.
106	220	small pearl	The sugar boils in the pan and forms small, pearl-like balls.
109	228	large pearl	The 'pearls' are better formed and separated.
112	234	small soufflé	Dip a skimmer into the sugar syrup and blow across the holes; small sugar balls will be blown off.
114	237	large soufflé	Test as above; the sugar will form larger bubbles.
118	244	small ball	Dip your finger into cold water, then into the sugar syrup. Plunge immediately into cold water; the sugar will slide off your finger and be soft enough to roll into a ball.
120	248	medium ball	The sugar balls are harder and more resistant.
124	255	large ball	As medium ball.
135	275	light crack	Dip your finger into cold water, then into the sugar syrup. Plunge into cold water; a sliver of sugar will fall off your finger.
144	291	crack	Test as above; a larger piece of sugar will slide off your finger.
152	306	hard crack	Test as above; the sugar will slide off your finger and shatter when it touches the water.

SUCRE COULE
(Poured sugar)

· INGREDIENTS ·

1 kg/2 lb 2 oz beet sugar
or cane sugar cubes

400 ml/14 fl oz water

250 g/9 oz glucose

Food colourings, as
appropriate

1 tbsp peanut oil *or* pure
vaseline, for greasing

Royal icing
(see page 236) (optional)

Pinch of cornflour

*Preparation time: about 20
minutes*

*Cooking time: about 25
minutes*

Models made from *sucre coulé* are quite stunning — like stained glass windows. Place them on a platter with a special dessert for an occasion, or feature them on a buffet or at a banquet.

Although these models are not difficult to make, they do require a great deal of application and, above all, time.

· OUTLINING THE MODEL AND ITS BASE ·

The model and base must be prepared with the utmost care and attention. First of all, draw and cut out templates of your chosen model and its base, using either pliable or rigid paper. The base must be sufficiently large and well-proportioned to give the model a very stable support. It can be any shape — oval, round, rectangular etc.

When the templates are ready, on a wooden or formica surface, lightly dusted with cornflour, roll out the modelling paste to a thickness of between 5-7 mm/¼-⅓ in, depending on the size of your model. The larger the model, the thicker the paste should be to make it more solid.

Place the template on the paste and, using the point of a small knife, cut around the edges. Remove the template, then the cut-out model. Take great care not to spoil the edges, which must be very smooth.

Using another piece of modelling paste, prepare the base in the same way. Lay a sheet of foil on the marble slab or baking sheet, taking care not to crumple it. Carefully place the prepared modelling paste on the foil. Use the templates to check that the edges have not stretched.

With a small brush, grease the inside edges of the paste with oil or melted vaseline. The paste is now ready for the sugar.

At this point you can, if you wish, pipe out some decorations in royal icing. This will add interest and life to your model. Use a paper cone or piping bag fitted with a 2 mm/¹⁄₁₆ in nozzle.

If you are adding this decoration, leave the piped icing to dry on the foil for at least 4 hours before pouring the sugar, otherwise it will swell and disintegrate when it comes into contact with the hot sugar.

· PREPARATION AND COOKING ·

Pour the water into the pan, then add the sugar. Stir gently with a small skimmer. When the sugar has dissolved slightly, set the pan over a gentle heat and stir until the sugar has dissolved completely.

Once it begins to bubble, it will throw out a kind of white

· EQUIPMENT ·

Copper sugar pan

Sugar thermometer

Marble slab or *an absolutely
smooth, flat work surface or
baking sheet*

Small paintbrush

Aluminium foil

Modelling paste, plasticine
or *confectioners' rulers*, or *a
metal strip which is pliable
enough to be bent into any
shape*

Gas jet (optional)

PICTURE PAGES 230-1

Continued overleaf

1

2

1
On a surface lightly dusted with cornflour, roll out the modelling paste or plasticine to a thickness of 5–7 mm/¼–⅓ in, using wooden rulers to measure the thickness accurately.

2
Place the templates on the plasticine and cut round them with a sharp knife, keeping the knife vertical. Carefully lift out the plasticine shapes.

3

4

3
Lay the prepared plasticine on smooth foil. Use the templates to check that the edges have not stretched. Oil the inner edges of the plasticine.

4
Cook the sugar and add colourings. Stand the pan on a wooden trivet for 1½ minutes to cool the sugar and burst the air bubbles. Pour into the model and base.

5

6

5
Make 1 cut in the plasticine and lift it away from the sugar models when set. Gently scrape away any plasticine which sticks with a sharp knife.

6
Leave the model and base to cool for several hours, then pipe on any decoration in royal icing. When the icing is dry, assemble the model and base.

foam. Skim this carefully off the surface until it is completely clean, taking care to rinse the skimmer well each time in a bowl of very clean water.

Use your fingertips to brush down the inside of the pan, dipping them into cold water each time, or use a perfectly clean pastry brush dipped into cold water. This will prevent the unmelted sugar from sticking to the sides of the pan and crystallizing. The crystals might also fall back into the boiling sugar and cause it to recrystallize. It can also cause the sugar to lose its transparency once it has been poured.

Add the glucose and partially cover the pan with a very clean lid. Cook the sugar over high heat.

Place the thermometer in the sugar; add any colourings when the temperature reaches about 140°C/284°F. When it reaches 156°C/312°F, take the pan off the heat.

Stand the pan on a wooden trivet for 1½ minutes so that the sugar cools very slightly before pouring, and to allow most of the small air bubbles to escape.

· POURING THE SUGAR ·

Pour the sugar in a regular, continuous stream into the cut-out template in the modelling paste until it reaches the top of the paste. Should any air bubbles appear, and you want a completely smooth surface, gently blow them away immediately with a gas jet wherever they appear, or prick them quickly with the point of a very fine knife, wiping the knife carefully each time.

Leave to cool for about 20 minutes; the edges of the sugar should have begun to harden. Lift off the modelling paste; having been oiled, it will peel away easily. If any should stick, gently scrape it away with the point of a knife. Leave the model to cool completely for 3 or 4 hours. You can then carefully peel off the foil and attach the model to the base.

To attach the model, dip the very bottom, for one second only, into some hard crack sugar, then immediately stick it onto the base; or, using a small spoon or paper cone, pipe a fine line of hard crack sugar round the perimeter of the base and quickly set the model on top. In either case, hold it down for 2 or 3 minutes, so that it sticks firmly to the base.

· NOTES ·

You can use a pliable metal strip or confectioners' rulers instead of modelling paste; oil the inside edges before pouring in the sugar.

To keep your models transparent and brilliant, spray a thin film of clear varnish over the models and bases as soon as they are cold. This will also protect them from damp, dust and fingerprints etc. and will preserve them for several days.

SUCRE FILE
(Spun sugar)

· INGREDIENTS ·

250 g/9 oz sugar

90 ml/3½ fl oz water

65 g/2½ oz glucose

1 tbsp peanut oil *or* pure
vaseline, for greasing

Preparation time: 5 minutes

Cooking time: about 15
minutes

Spun sugar, which is so easy to make, is chiefly used for decoration. Its delicate, brilliant quality gives a festive air to *pièces montées* or *Soufflé glacé aux fraises* (page 178), iced desserts and sorbets and to our *Igloo Douillet* (see page 108). Since it is supple and pliable, spun sugar can be bent into all sorts of attractive shapes.

· PREPARATION AND COOKING ·

Pour the water into the pan, then add the sugar. Stir gently with a small skimmer. As soon as the sugar has dissolved slightly, set the pan over a gentle heat and stir until the sugar has dissolved completely and begins to boil.

Once it starts to bubble, it will throw out a kind of white foam. Skim this off the surface several times, using a skimmer, taking care to rinse it well each time in a bowl of very clean water.

Use your fingertips to clean the inside of the pan, dipping them into cold water each time, or use a scrupulously clean pastry brush dipped in cold water. This will prevent the unmelted sugar from sticking to the sides of the pan and crystallizing. The crystals might fall back into the boiling sugar and cause it to recrystallize.

Add the glucose, partially cover the pan with a very clean lid and cook the sugar over high heat.

Place the thermometer in the sugar. When the temperature reaches 152°C/305°F, take the pan off the heat and rest it on a wooden board for 2 minutes to cool and thicken.

If the sugar is too hot, it will fall in little drops, but will not spin; if it is too cold, it will be very difficult to spin.

· PREPARING THE WORK AREA ·

Lay several sheets of greaseproof paper on the floor to protect it. Balance a lightly oiled broom handle across two chairs or stools, or use an oiled rolling pin, holding one end carefully in your hand.

· SPINNING THE SUGAR ·

Dip the prongs of the forks or whisk into the sugar and flick them rapidly backwards and forwards above the rolling pin or broom handle. The sugar will run down and spin into fine threads on both sides. Continue to 'throw' the sugar in this way until the broom handle or rolling pin is moderately well covered. Do not overfill it with too many threads. Collect up

· EQUIPMENT ·

Copper sugar pan

Sugar thermometer

2 forks or a small balloon
whisk, with the rounded
ends cut off

4 sheets of greaseproof paper

Rolling pin or broom
handle

all the sugar threads (or 'Angel's hair') and place on a lightly oiled baking tray, if you are going to use them within an hour. To keep it for any length of time, pack in an airtight container lined with silica gel, quicklime or carbide covered with foil. It can be stored for up to 2 days.

· NOTES ·

Spun sugar very easily picks up moisture from the atmosphere and softens, so if you have to work in a humid atmosphere for any reason, leave sugar spinning until another day.

Spun sugar is also used to make the stamens of sugar flowers. Gently roll a handful into a sausage shape about 2 cm/1 in diameter. Squeeze in the base to 4-5 mm/about ¼ in diameter and, with a heated knife, cut off about 3-4 cm/1½ in, taking care that the other end remains open. Dip the open end into crystallized sugar, tinted pink, yellow, or whatever colour you like. Repeat the process as often as necessary. You can keep the finished stamens in an airtight box containing a dehydrating compound.

SUCRE ROCHER
(Rock sugar)

PICTURE PAGE 230

· INGREDIENTS ·
500 g/1 lb 1 oz beet sugar *or* cane sugar cubes
200 ml/7 fl oz water
1 tbsp Royal icing (see page 236)
Food colourings (optional)

Preparation time: 5 minutes
Cooking time: about 20 minutes

· EQUIPMENT ·
Copper sugar pan, large enough to hold 3 times the given quantities
Sugar thermometer
Aluminium foil
1 soufflé dish *or* bowl

Unlike other sugars, *sucre rocher* keeps very well exposed to the air, and it is very simple to make. It adds an unusual decorative touch, and can be embellished with flowers made from pulled sugar. As its name implies, *sucre rocher* can be used to give a very attractive rocky effect.

· PREPARATION AND COOKING ·

Preheat the oven to 120°C/250°F/gas 1. Line the soufflé dish or bowl with foil. Pour the water into the pan, then add the sugar and stir gently with a small skimmer. When the sugar has dissolved slightly, set the pan over a gentle heat and stir until the sugar has dissolved completely and begins to boil.

Once it begins to bubble, it will throw out a kind of white foam. Skim this off the surface several times, using a skimmer, taking care to rinse it well each time in a bowl of very clean water.

Use your fingertips to clean the inside of the pan, dipping them into cold water each time, or use a pristine clean pastry brush dipped into cold water. This will prevent the unmelted sugar from sticking to the sides of the pan and crystallizing. The crystals might fall back into the boiling sugar and make it grainy or cause it to recrystallize.

Partially cover the pan with a very clean lid and cook the

sugar over high heat. Place the thermometer in the sugar; add any colourings when the temperature reaches about 120°C/248°F. When it reaches 138°C/280°F, take the pan off the heat and, with a scrupulously clean wooden spatula, very quickly stir in the royal icing. Mix well, but do not overwork. The sugar will now rise and almost double in volume (hence the need for a large pan!) Do not stir while the sugar is rising. It will fall and then rise again. As it begins to rise for the second time, quickly pour it into the prepared dish, where it will finish rising.

· DRYING THE 'SUCRE ROCHER' ·

As soon as the sugar is in the dish, place it immediately in the preheated oven for 10 minutes, so that it does not fall again and will harden. Put the sugar, still in the dish, in a dry place and leave it for about 12 hours.

· FINISHING ·

After 12 hours, turn the sugar out of the dish and remove the foil. With a serrated knife, cut off the crumbly outer crust.

Depending on what you intend to make, cut the sugar with a fretsaw, or break it into pieces by tapping it lightly with the back of a large knife. You can also file it down if you want a fairly flat, smooth surface.

The sugar is now ready to use.

· DECORATION ·

Colour this sugar during cooking for a pretty, smooth effect. If, however, you want to give your imagination full rein and are aiming for subtle reflections and highlighted reliefs, it is best to use an atomizer or spray. Spray-on colours are added after the model is completely finished.

Assemble and stick together various pieces with a little royal icing. You must leave the finished model to dry for at least 12 hours.

If you want a lighter, more crumbly sugar, add a touch more royal icing.

SUCRE SOUFFLE
(Blown sugar)

· INGREDIENTS ·

1 kg/2 lb 2 oz beet sugar
or cane sugar cubes

400 ml/14 fl oz water

250 g/9 oz glucose

1 tbsp peanut oil *or* pure
vaseline, for greasing

Food colourings, as
appropriate (optional)

*Preparation time: 5 minutes,
plus making the shapes*

*Cooking time: about 25
minutes*

· PREPARATION ·

Pour the water into the pan, then add the sugar. Stir with a skimmer. As soon as the sugar has dissolved a little, set the pan over a gentle heat and stir until the sugar has dissolved completely and begins to boil.

Once it starts to bubble, it will throw out a kind of white foam. Skim this off the surface until completely clean, rinsing the skimmer well in a bowl of very clean water each time.

Use your fingertips to clean the inside of the pan, dipping them into cold water each time, or use a scrupulously clean pastry brush dipped in cold water.

Add the glucose, partially cover the pan with a very clean lid and cook the sugar over high heat.

Insert the sugar thermometer and cook until the temperature reaches 150°C/302°F. Take the pan off the heat and stand it on a wooden trivet for 30 seconds. During the cooking process, up to 140°C/284°F, the sugar will discolour a little and should take on a slightly yellow tint. This will provide the ideal base colour for painting the models and will help in obtaining the deeper and more vivid colours.

· COOLING THE SUGAR ·

Pour the sugar onto a spotlessly clean oiled marble slab or the tefal sheet. Use a lightly oiled palette knife or metal scraper to fold the edges back on themselves 3 or 4 times, until they have almost stopped spreading.

· 'SATINIZING' THE SUGAR ·

Leaving the sugar on the marble, fold the mass back onto itself with your fingertips or the palette knife. Start to pull it 5 or 6 times. The sugar should now be cool enough to handle. Place one hand on one end of the mass and pull it out, then fold it back on itself. Do this 20-30 times, alternating the direction each time, until the sugar becomes very glossy and smooth. Place the sugar on the plastic sheet under the lamp, or stand it in a sieve or on a baking sheet just inside the open oven, which you have preheated to 120°C/250°F/gas 1.

· BLOWING THE SUGAR ·

Now the sugar is satinized, cut off a ball large enough to make your desired shape. This ball should be at a uniform temperature, still warm and firm but malleable.

Dig your thumb into the centre to make a cavity. Heat the end of an aluminium tube or the nozzle of the pump so that

· EQUIPMENT ·

Copper sugar pan

Sugar thermometer

Marble slab or *a tefal sheet,
60 × 40 cm/24 × 16 in*

Palette knife or *metal
scraper*

Sugar lamp

Thick, heatproof plastic sheet
or *a sieve* or *baking sheet*

Aluminium tubes or *a
sugar-blowing pump*

Small electric fan

Foam rubber mat

Small paintbrushes

PICTURE PAGES 230-1

the sugar will stick to it, then insert it halfway into the cavity. With your fingertips, firmly press the edges of the sugar around the end of the tube or nozzle so that it sticks.

Blow in air gently and regularly, so that the sugar ball swells; make sure that the thickness remains constant and even throughout the operation. Use your hands to support the swelling bubble and, with your fingertips, begin to form your shapes. Blow constantly while you do this, just enough to maintain the air pressure inside the sugar ball.

When you have achieved your desired size and shape, mark the shape as you wish; for example, roll it over a grater or hard bristle brush, or mark it with the back of a large knife to look like a peach. To imitate the bloom on a peach skin, just roll the blown and painted sugar peach in a plate of cornflour. To make an animal's paws or tail, cut out the shape with scissors.

Place the finished object in front of a small fan or in a relatively cold place. Never put it directly onto a flat surface, or it will lose its shape. Heat the blade of a small knife over a gas flame, then carefully cut the sugar cord between the model and the tube or nozzle. Place the sugar model on a piece of foam rubber so that it does not break.

· NOTES ·

If you wish, you can paint the finished models with food colouring — give your artistic imagination full rein! All kinds of fruits and animals can be created in sugar, some very simple, others more complex.

Once the sugar is satinized, it can be divided into 4 with a large knife. Use only 1 piece for the *sucre soufflé;* the others may be kept until needed in an airtight container lined with quicklime, carbide or silica gel covered with foil. Then you need only reheat them under a lamp or at the opening of an oven preheated to 120°C/250°F, turning from time to time, so that the sugar softens evenly as it warms.

If you want to keep a high gloss on the finished sugar pieces, spray each one with an aerosol lacquer. This will also protect them from quick deterioration.

SUCRE TIRE
(Pulled sugar)

· INGREDIENTS ·

1 kg/2 lb 2 oz beet sugar
or cane sugar cubes

500 ml/18 fl oz water

1.5 g/scant ½ tsp
cream of tartar

1 tbsp peanut oil *or* pure
vaseline, for greasing

Food colourings
(optional)

*Preparation time: 5 minutes,
plus making the decoration*

*Cooking time: about 25
minutes*

· PREPARATION AND COOKING ·

Pour the water into the pan, then add the sugar and cream of tartar. Stir with a skimmer. When the sugar has dissolved a little, set the pan over a gentle heat and stir until the sugar has dissolved completely and is beginning to boil.

Once the sugar begins to bubble, it will throw out a kind of white foam. Skim this off the surface until completely clean, taking care to rinse the skimmer well in a bowl of very clean water each time.

Use your fingertips to clean the inside of the pan, dipping them into cold water each time, or use a scrupulously clean pastry brush dipped into cold water. This will prevent the unmelted sugar from sticking to the sides of the pan and crystallizing. The crystals might fall back into the boiling sugar and become granular and the grains may show when the sugar is pulled.

Partially cover the pan with a very clean lid and cook the sugar over high heat.

Place the thermometer in the sugar; add any colourings

· EQUIPMENT ·

Copper sugar pan

Sugar thermometer

*Marble slab or tefal sheet,
60 × 40 cm/24 × 16 in*

*Palette knife or metal
scraper*

*Thick, heatproof plastic sheet
or a sieve or small baking
sheet*

Sugar lamp

*A set of modelling sticks and
pastry-cutters on which to
rest the flowers*

*Gas jet or small spirit lamp
for sticking together leaves
and petals*

PICTURE PAGES 230-1

1
Pour the cooked sugar on to a spotlessly clean oiled marble slab and with a palette knife fold the hot sugar mass back on to itself.

2
With your fingertips start to pull the sugar 5 or 6 times.

3
When it has cooled sufficiently, place a hand on one end of the sugar and pull it out. Fold it back on itself and repeat 35-40 times until very glossy and smooth ('satinized').

4
Cut the satinized sugar into 6 or 8 pieces. Work with only 1 piece at a time; store the rest in an airtight container with a dehumidifying agent.

5

Place the satinized sugar under a sugar lamp and begin to pull and mould it into the desired shape.

5

6

Break off small pieces of the sugar to form flower petals. eg: for roses or carnations.

6

7

Use sugar tinted with different food colourings during the cooking stage to make petals, leaves etc.

7

8

As you finish each petal or leaf, rest it on a pastry cutter so as not to spoil the shape while you are moulding the next one. You will need at least 27 petals to make a perfect rose.

8

9

To finish, use your fingertips to mould the petals into elaborate flower shapes.

9

10

Carnation: you can also use modelling sticks to form a variety of leaf and petal shapes.

10

11

Heat the ends of the petals with a gas jet before assembling the finished flower.

12

Add extra texture to the petals by marking them with the bristles of a brush.

11

12

when the temperature reaches about 140°C/284°F. When it reaches 156°C/312°F, take the pan off the heat and stand it on a trivet for 30 seconds, or plunge the base into iced water for 5 seconds.

· COOLING THE SUGAR ·

Pour the sugar onto a spotlessly clean oiled or greased marble slab, or onto the tefal sheet. Use a lightly oiled palette knife or metal scraper to fold the edges back on themselves 3 or 4 times, until they have almost stopped spreading.

· 'SATINIZING' THE SUGAR ·

Leaving the sugar on the marble, fold the mass back onto itself with your fingertips or the palette knife. Start to pull it 5 or 6 times.

By now, the heat of the sugar will be more bearable and you can hold it in your hands and begin the satinizing process properly. Place one hand on one end of the mass and pull it out, then fold it back on itself. Do this 35 or 40 times, alternating the direction each time, until the sugar becomes very glossy and smooth. It will make cracking sounds, known as 'singing.' It is now ready for moulding.

Place the sugar on the plastic sheet under the lamp, or stand it on a sieve or baking sheet inside the opening of the oven, which you have preheated to 120°C/250°F/gas 1. Now cut off a ball large enough for the shape you want; work with only 1 piece at a time, pulling and moulding the sugar into the desired shape.

· NOTES ·

Once the sugar mass has become satiny, it can be cut into 6 or 8 pieces with a cook's knife. The unused pieces, once they have cooled, can be kept until needed in an airtight box lined with silica gel, carbide or quicklime covered with aluminium foil. Then you need only reheat them under the lamp, or at the opening of the preheated oven, turning from time to time so that the sugar softens evenly as it warms.

A tefal sheet is less effective than a marble slab for cooling cooked sugar. If you haven't got a marble, it is better to cook a smaller quantity of sugar.

PRESENTATION

Decorations must always be neat and very simple. They must never dominate or take over the dessert. Their rôle is to delight the eye and titillate the tastebuds; sometimes, they serve to highlight a special occasion, such as a christening or birthday.

Some decorative motifs can be prepared hours or even days in advance. Store them well away from any heat or damp. These embellishments (called *décors rapportés*) are made separately and added to the dessert or *pièce montée* just before serving. They add a more sophisticated touch than the *décors appliqués*, which are applied directly to the dessert at the last moment.

PATE A CHOUX A DECOR
(Decorative choux paste)

· INGREDIENTS ·

35 g/1½ oz butter, cut
into small pieces
50 ml/2 fl oz water
50 ml/2 fl oz milk
Pinch of salt
60 g/2 oz flour
2 × 50-55 g/size 5 eggs

Makes about 300 g/10 oz
Preparation time: 20
minutes
Cooking time: 6-10 minutes,
depending on the size of the
decorations

You can use these decorations to complement various desserts and sorbets.

· PREPARATION ·

Preheat the oven to 160°C/320°F/gas 4.
Cooking the paste: Cook exactly as for *Pâte à choux*, (see page 54) but stir in the flour with a wire whisk instead of a spatula and dry out the paste, using a spatula, for only 30 seconds.

Beat in the eggs, one at a time, then pass the paste through a very fine sieve, rubbing it through with a plastic scraper into a bowl. Set aside.

Piping the paste: Line a baking sheet with baking parchment or buttered greaseproof paper and pipe out the paste into your desired shape — chequerboard, pine trees, fish net, seashell etc.

Bake in the preheated oven for 6-10 minutes. For shells or any raised shapes, pipe them out flat, bake and, as soon as they come out of the oven, mould them around a spherical mould, or whatever shape is appropriate. Leave to cool on the mould.

· STORAGE ·

Pâte à choux will keep very well for a week in a dry, airtight container.

· EQUIPMENT ·

1 saucepan
1 fine sieve
Piping bag with a plain
2-3 mm/¹/₁₆-¹/₈ in nozzle, or
a paper cone
Greaseproof paper or baking
parchment
1 baking sheet

MAIN PICTURE *Floral presentation in pulled sugar*
LEFT, TOP TO BOTTOM *Madame Fish: poured sugar over royal icing piped on to paper; Rabbit: poured sugar with decoration piped in royal icing; Pink flamingo: pastillage; Cottage: pastillage.*

RIGHT, TOP TO BOTTOM *Fruit bowl: bunch of grapes and vine leaf, pear, apple, lemon and banana in blown sugar; Penguin waiter in blown sugar; Fish in blown sugar on rock sugar, with a poured sugar base; Sugar cubes and rock sugar.*

RIGHT *'Stained glass window', Village in a landscape: design piped on to paper and dried.*

PASTILLAGE
(Gum sugar paste)

PICTURE PAGES 230-1

· INGREDIENTS ·

500 g/1 lb 1 oz icing
sugar, sifted

50 g/2 oz cornflour,
sifted

1 tbsp lukewarm water

1 egg white

2 leaves of gelatine,
soaked in cold water for
15 minutes, then drained

Juice of ½ lemon,
strained

Pinch of arrowroot

Pinch of icing sugar

Makes about 650 g/1 lb 6 oz

· EQUIPMENT ·

Smooth wooden board

Bain-marie

Sheet of polythene

*Very smooth rolling pin,
preferably plastic*

1 or more very sharp knives

1 baking sheet

Making *pastillage* does not require much experience, but you do need nimble fingers for cutting out and moulding. In culinary competitions, one often sees models which have taken thousands of hours to prepare — cathedrals, temples, Eiffel Towers etc. Sometimes, *pastillage* is made with gum arabic instead of gelatine which is why it is called 'gum' sugar paste.

· PREPARATION ·

Place the sifted icing sugar and starch on a wooden surface and make a well in the centre. Pour in the lukewarm water.

Put the egg white in a bain-marie and heat gently, stirring with your fingertips, so that it does not coagulate. Remove from the bain-marie and stir in the well-drained gelatine until completely dissolved. Still stirring with your fingertips, pour this mixture into the well, add the lemon juice and knead together, gradually drawing the icing sugar and starch into the centre. You should have a firm but malleable paste. If it seems too soft, add a little more icing sugar; if it seems too firm, add a drop of lukewarm water.

Immediately wrap the *pastillage* in a sheet of polythene so that it does not dry out or crack.

· SHAPING ·

If possible, this should be done on a very smooth, clean wooden table, dusted with arrowroot.

Roll out the *pastillage* to the appropriate size, shape and thickness for the model; use a template to help you if you like.

· DRYING ·

Immediately place the shaped model on a very smooth baking sheet lightly dusted with icing sugar and leave to dry at room temperature for 24-48 hours. Once the top is dry, turn the model over so that the bottom also dries. The drier the *pastillage*, the more solid the model will be.

For a really smooth finish like porcelain, polish the surface with very fine glasspaper.

· TO SERVE ·

You can make several pieces to fashion one larger model (eg, our little house, page 230). Stick the pieces together with royal icing (see page 236), piped out with a paper cone.

Pastillage painted with food colouring looks very attractive and artistic on a buffet table; it is also very simple to do. If you like, you can also colour the *pastillage* during kneading.

· STORAGE ·

Pastillage will not keep for long; it will dry out and crack. For best results, shape it immediately after kneading. It will, however, keep for up to 24 hours in the fridge if you wrap it well in polythene.

N O U G A T I N E

· INGREDIENTS ·

480 g/1 lb flaked almonds

660 g/1 lb 6 oz sugar

60 g/2 oz butter (optional)

2 tbsp peanut oil

Makes 1.2 kg/2 lb 12 oz

Preparation time: 25 minutes

· EQUIPMENT ·

1 baking sheet

1 baking sheet or a plastic or marble board

1 sugar pan

Weighted or hardwood rolling pin

Pastry cutters, flan rings or a chopping knife, depending on the desired shape

Sugar lamp (optional)

Little *nougatine* shapes (squares, lozenges etc) make a delightful accompaniment to coffee. Serve them with other petits fours. Dip one side in chocolate for a perfect finishing touch.

· PREPARATION ·

Preheat the oven to 180°C/350°F/gas 5.

Have ready all the cutters and implements you will need for shaping the *nougatine*.

· TO COOK ·

Spread the flaked almonds over a baking sheet and place in the preheated oven until very lightly browned. Put the sugar in the pan, set over low heat and cook until melted and light golden, stirring gently and continuously with a spatula, then stir in the almonds.

Stir over low heat for 1 minute, then add the butter if you are using it; it will give the *nougatine* an extra sheen but is not essential. Mix until the butter is completely absorbed.

Pour the mixture onto a lightly oiled baking sheet.

· SHAPING THE NOUGATINE ·

Place the baking sheet near the warm oven, keeping the oven door half open; if it is not placed near a source of heat, the *nougatine* will become difficult to work. Work with only 1 piece at a time, using the appropriate size for the shape you want. Roll out each piece on a lightly oiled, warmed baking sheet, or on a plastic board or lightly oiled marble. You must work very quickly, since the *nougatine* quickly becomes brittle.

Roll it to an appropriate thickness to the desired shape, but never thicker than 5 mm/¼ in.

Quickly cut out the shapes with the cutters, or the blade or heel of a knife. If you are moulding the *nougatine*, do this very fast, so that it follows the shape and contours of the mould. Do not unmould before the *nougatine* is completely cold.

Continued on page 236

Cat (120 g/4 oz pink almond paste).

Owl (120 g/4 oz green almond paste).

Spotted dog (105 g/3½ oz untinted and 15 g/½ oz light brown almond paste). Marzipan is tinted with liquid food colouring. The eyes are Royal icing, pupils, ears and feet are dipped in chocolate.

MODELLING IN MARZIPAN AND ALMOND PASTE

Rose (40-50 g/1½ oz red almond paste).

Marzipan seals, tinted and painted a strong blue; base and icebergs are coloured poured sugar.

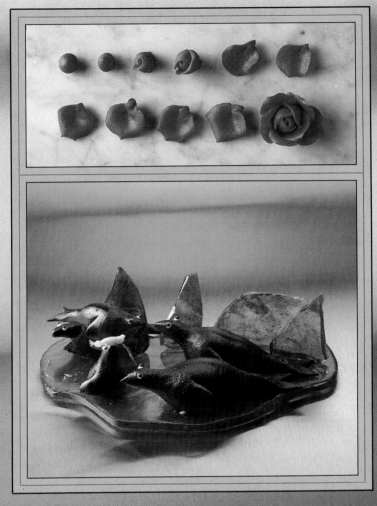

Marzipan pieces should be brushed with cocoa butter to protect against dust and fingerprints, and to give an attractive sheen.

If you have a sugar lamp, place just far enough from the *nougatine* to keep the whole mass warm while you mould individual pieces. Any small leftover pieces can be reheated in the oven and used again.

· STORAGE ·

Like all sugar-based confectionery, *nougatine* dislikes humidity, and therefore keeps for only a day or two in damp conditions.

· NOTES ·

You can use nibbed almonds instead of flaked, but they look less attractive.

Pieces of *nougatine* can be stuck together with hard crack sugar to make all sorts of artistic shapes and designs. To make a really classic *nougatine* sculpture, pipe out a pattern with royal icing.

GLACE ROYALE
(Royal icing)

· INGREDIENTS ·

50 g/2 oz egg whites

250 g/9 oz icing sugar, sifted

Juice of ¼ lemon, strained

Preparation time: 5 minutes

· PREPARATION ·

Put the egg whites into the bowl and, beating at low speed, add the sifted sugar, a little at a time, then the lemon juice. Beat until the icing is firm and has risen slightly. It is ready if, when you turn the whisk, the icing forms a fine, straight point and holds its shape whichever way you turn the whisk.

If the icing is too thick, so that a point does not form, add a touch more egg white. If it is too liquid and the point flops over when you hold it upwards, add a little more icing sugar.

· STORAGE ·

Royal icing keeps very well in an airtight plastic container or in a bowl covered with a damp cloth, which will prevent it from drying out and forming a crust. It will keep in the fridge for several days, although it is better to use it immediately.

· NOTES ·

Use a palette knife to spread the icing thinly on pastry matchsticks (see page 198) to serve with coffee, or pipe it into all sorts of decorative shapes using a piping bag. You can also use it to assemble *sucre rocher* creations (see page 222).

Royal icing can be tinted with a little food colouring to brighten up petits fours and decorations.

· EQUIPMENT ·

Electric mixer, with a paddle or *a mixing bowl and wire whisk*

Inspiration for the shapes of letters and words in Royal icing (opposite page) can be drawn from many sources. Book jackets and food packaging are readily available and encompass both traditional and contemporary motifs. Examples here include English and Roman scripts, bookface, Art deco and fantasy designs.

A series of decorative borders in Royal icing add the finishing touches to such desserts as Le Fraisier (page 114) and Croquembouche (page 126).

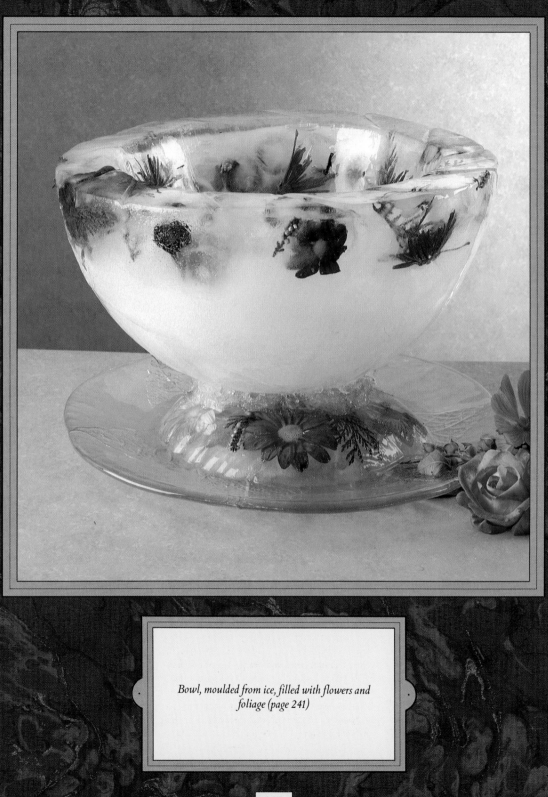

Bowl, moulded from ice, filled with flowers and
foliage (page 241)

FEATHERING

A decorative motif that relies for effect on contrasting colours, a steady hand, and a very finely pointed knife or cocktail stick. Combinations of Melba sauce, melted chocolate, double cream, caramel sauce and chocolate sauce decorate a variety of bases: ABOVE LEFT *Melba sauce, and* RIGHT *Caramel sauce (page 64).* BELOW LEFT *Chocolate sauce (page 67), and* RIGHT *Peach coulis (page 71).*

PATE A DECOR
(Decorative cornets)

· INGREDIENTS ·
60 g/2 oz flour

60 g/2 oz icing sugar

1 white from a 70 g/ size 1 egg *or* 1½ whites from 2 × 50 g/size 5 eggs

In our restaurants we like to present the sorbets in these enchanting cornets, but take care because, like all delicate and elegant objects, they are very fragile.

This mixture can also be used for piping all sorts of decorative shapes — pine trees, fences, little houses or birds, using a very small nozzle.

· EQUIPMENT ·
1 template with diagram

Piping bag or paper cones, fitted with a plain 2 mm/¹⁄₁₆ in nozzle

Baking sheet

Baking parchment or greaseproof paper

1

2

1
Butter and flour a baking sheet. Press the template, design side downwards, on to the baking sheet to impress the design on the flour. Leave space between each impression.

2
Pipe the mixture around the edge of the design, then make a mark in the centre and pipe 2 V-shapes on either side, then 2 inverted V-shapes. Also pipe serpentines for the bases.

3
Add more water to the mixture to make a thick liquid paste. With a small palette knife, fill in the bases of the cornets with this paste.

4
Bake for 2-3 minutes, then carefully bend the mixture into cornet shapes.

5
Carefully place the cornets inside dariole moulds, lattice side down, and leave to harden.

6
Dip the bases of the cornets into hard crack sugar and gently stick them on to the solid part of the serpentine 'feet'.

3

4

5

6

Makes 8-10 cornets
Preparation time: 25
minutes
Cooking time: 3 minutes

· PREPARATION ·

Preheat the oven to 220°C/425°F/gas 8.

The mixture: Sift the flour and icing sugar into a bowl. Add the egg white and work together with a spatula until completely amalgamated. Cover the bowl with a damp cloth and refrigerate for at least 30 minutes before using the mixture. This resting time is essential, but you can make the mixture in advance and keep it in the fridge, covered with clingfilm, for up to 24 hours.

· TO COOK ·

Pipe out the mixture onto a baking sheet lined with baking parchment or buttered greaseproof paper. Depending on the size and shape of your model, bake in the preheated oven for 3-5 minutes.

You will need to add enough cold water to the mixture to make a thick liquid paste before piping the bases.

COUPE EN GLACE MOULEE
(How to mould a bowl out of ice)

Put some ice cubes in the larger bowl, then place the smaller bowl on top. Pour some iced water into the gap between the bowls, then put in some brightly coloured flowers and foliage and add more ice cubes, making sure that they hold down the flowers and foliage and prevent them from rising to the surface.

Continue until the space between the bowls is filled. Now weigh down the smaller bowl to stop it from floating and to keep it at the correct height. Freeze for 6-24 hours until solid.

To unmould, remove the weights from the smaller bowl and pour in a little lukewarm water (no hotter than 30°C/86°F). Remove the smaller bowl after 1 or 2 minutes.

Dip the bottom of the larger bowl into lukewarm water and carefully unmould it. You now have a bowl made of ice in which to serve fruit sorbets in their skin — pineapple, for example — or scoops of ice cream. If you are serving ice cream, first line the bowl with foil. If you like, you can stick the bowl onto a stand also moulded from ice; use finely crushed ice to attach the bowl to the stand. The edge of the bowl can be decorated in a zig-zag pattern by marking with the back of a knife dipped in boiling water between each cut.

Just before serving, place the bowl on a napkin to absorb the moisture as it melts. It will last at room temperature for about 30 minutes or more, depending on the size.

· EQUIPMENT ·
2 freezerproof hemispherical moulds, 1 two-thirds smaller than the other
Ice cubes
Flowers and foliage

PICTURE PAGE 238

C O P E A U X   D E   C H O C O L A T
(Chocolate curls)

Chocolate curls make an attractive decoration for many desserts, including *Oeufs à la neige* (page 105). They can be made with either plain or white chocolate or, for an unusual 2-tone effect, you can combine them. Spread some dark chocolate on the slab and just before it sets comb it with a pastry comb. Coat with a thin layer of white chocolate. Once this has hardened, proceed as for Step 2 (below).

1

Pour the melted chocolate on to a chilled, dry marble slab. Spread it thinly backwards and forwards and from side to side, with a palette knife, until the chocolate sets.

2

With a large knife at a 30° angle, push the chocolate away from you, gradually straightening the knife until it is at 90° to the slab. The sharper the angle, the smaller the curls.

3

To make petals pull a plain 10 cm/4 in pastry cutter across the chocolate towards you.

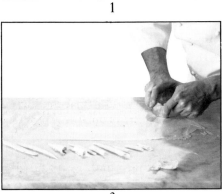

4

Dip the base of each petal into melted chocolate and place one petal on top of the other to form a flower.

1

2

3

4

GLOSSARY OF PATISSERIE TERMS

Abaisser:
To roll out pastry.

Abricoter:
To apply a thin, even layer or coating of apricot jam, redcurrant jelly, etc with a brush.

Appareil:
The mixture of ingredients used in the preparation of a dish (eg, *appareil à soufflé*: soufflé mixture).

Apprêt:
The time needed for a leavened mixture to rise and ferment between the preparation and the baking.

Beurrer:
To brush the inside of a mould, or a baking sheet, with melted or softened butter. It also means placing the butter in puff pastry dough before rolling out.

Beurre clarifié (clarified butter):
To clarify, heat the butter very gently until it comes to the boil. Ladle the clear butter through a muslin-lined sieve leaving the milky deposit in the bottom of the pan.

Beurre noisette:
Bring some butter to the boil. When it stops foaming and just before it begins to colour, it gives off a wonderful, nutty scent.

Beurre pommade (softened butter):
Remove the butter from the fridge and leave in a warm place until softened.

Blanchir:
To whisk egg yolks and sugar vigorously together until light and foamy. (In pastry-making, this term has a different meaning from 'blanching' in cookery.)

Bloquer:
The point at which a chocolate coating becomes too thick to spread and then solidifies.

Carameliser:
To coat the inside of a mould with caramelized sugar; or to flavour a sauce or cream with caramelized sugar or liquid caramel.

Chemiser:
To line or coat the inside of a mould with a thick or thin layer of mixture (eg, a *bombe*), or with greaseproof paper.

Chiqueter:
To mark out the rim or edges of pastry dough (such as a *galette des rois*), by indenting diagonally with the blade of a knife; this ensures that the dough will rise uniformly and gives an attractive, tasteful decorative effect.

Concasser:
To pound or chop roughly.

Corser:
To give body to a dough or mixture so that it can be worked until it becomes firm and elastic.

Coucher or **dresser:**
To pipe choux pastry into various shapes using a forcing bag and nozzle (eg, choux buns or *éclairs*).

Cracher:
To cut or mark out incisions in puff pastry using a sharp knife; this is done, for example, with a *Pithiviers* so that it will develop properly during cooking.

Cuire à blanc (bake blind):
To bake pastry shells, flan cases, etc without a filling; the empty case is lined with greaseproof paper and filled with metal, ceramic or dried beans before baking.

Dessecher:
To evaporate moisture from a preparation (choux pastry, apple purée etc) by stirring over gentle heat.

Détailler:
To cut out pastry shapes with a pastry cutter (eg, tartlet cases or *fleurons*); or to divide a piece of dough into even-sized pieces (eg, bread dough).

Détrempe:
A dough mixture of flour, water, salt and sometimes, fat; sugar and butter are also added for croissants.

Dorer (to glaze):
To brush dough with beaten egg or eggwash made from egg yolk and milk before baking; this must be done very lightly.

Emincer:
To cut into very fine slices.

Enrober:
To cover a cake, sweet or petits fours completely with fondant, chocolate, icing, caramel, etc.

Fariner:
To dust a work surface with flour before rolling out pastry dough so that it will not stick; or to flour a greased mould lightly.

Foisonner:
To beat a mixture until it increases in volume (eg, ice cream).

Foncer:
To line a mould with pastry.

Fouetter:
To beat a fairly liquid mixture either in a machine or by hand.

Fraiser or **fraser:**
To work pastry ingredients with the palm of your hand to ensure that they are thoroughly mixed (eg, *pâte sucrée, pâte sablée* and shortcrust).

Glacer (to glaze):
To sprinkle a puff pastry dessert with icing sugar before putting it in a very hot oven for a few seconds to caramelize the sugar; or to ice a dessert or small choux pastries with a thin coating of fondant.

Macérer:
To steep dried, candied or fresh fruits in syrup, alcohol or liqueur so that they soak up the liquid and absorb its flavour and aroma.

Marbrer:
Fondant icing, decorated and marked with lines to look like marbling.

Masquer:
To use a palette knife to spread a smooth, even layer of cream over a dessert before adding the final decoration or icing.

Masse:
A mixture of several ingredients which will form the basis of a more elaborate dish (similar to *appareil*).

Meringuer:
To add a little sugar to fresh egg whites to strengthen the albumen and prevent them from breaking down; or to place a meringue-topped dessert in a very hot oven to give it an attractive colour.

Monder:
To skin almonds, walnuts, pistachios, etc and certain fresh fruits (eg, peaches) by pouring over boiling water for a few seconds, then refreshing in cold water.

Napper:
To cook until thick enough to coat a wooden spoon; *napper* denotes that a *crème anglaise* has reached the desired consistency; or to coat as in *abricoter*.

Paton:
A block of puff pastry during its preparation; any piece of dough of the correct size to use for a given recipe.

Pincer:
To pinch up the edges of a tart using your fingers or a pastry crimper.

Pointage:
The time between kneading a leavened dough and the first rising (the biological interaction of the yeast and sugar).

Pousse:
The development of a leavened dough caused by fermentation — the rising between kneading and baking.

Puncher:
To brush a *génoise* or sponge with alcohol-flavoured syrup.

Rognures:
The pastry trimmings left over from cutting out larger shapes. These may be used as flan cases or to make *mille-feuilles.*

Rompre (knock back):
With a lightly floured hand, lift up your risen dough and quickly flip it up 2 or 3 times; this will bring it back to its original volume.

Sabler:
To rub fat into flour with your fingertips until the mixture has a granular texture resembling fine breadcrumbs.

Sangler:
To pack a mixture of ice and salt around a mould filled with a *bombe* or other mixture to freeze it quickly.

Tabler:
To cool a chocolate coating once it has melted, while still keeping it at the right spreading consistency. This is done by working it on a marble slab with a palette knife or triangular scraper so that it does not harden and become lumpy (see also *bloquer*).

Travailler:
To beat a mixture with a whisk or spatula to make it smooth and homogenous.

Vanner:
To stir a sauce or cream occasionally while it is cooling, using a spatula. This prevents a skin from forming and the mixture from separating.

Zester:
To grate the rind of an orange or lemon with a cheese grater, or finely pare the zest with a zester, taking care to leave behind the bitter white pith.

· CONVERSION TABLES ·

Approximate equivalents		Liquid measurements	
Metric	Imperial	Metric	Imperial
15 g	$\frac{1}{2}$ oz	25 ml	1 fl oz
25–30 g	1 oz	50 ml	2 fl oz
40 g	$1\frac{1}{2}$ oz	100 ml	$3\frac{1}{2}$ fl oz
50–60 g	2 oz	125 ml	4 fl oz
75 g	$2\frac{1}{2}$ oz	150 ml	5 fl oz
100 g	$3\frac{1}{2}$ oz	200 ml	7 fl oz
125 g	4 oz	250 ml	9 fl oz
150 g	5 oz	275 ml	10 fl oz ($\frac{1}{2}$ pt)
200 g	7 oz	300 ml	11 fl oz
225 g	8 oz ($\frac{1}{2}$ lb)	350 ml	12 fl oz
300 g	10 oz	400 ml	14 fl oz
350 g	12 oz	450 ml	16 fl oz
400 g	13 oz	500 ml	18 fl oz
450 g	16 oz (1 lb)	575 ml	1 pt
500 g	17 oz	850 ml	$1\frac{1}{2}$ pt
900 g	2 lb	1 lt	$1\frac{3}{4}$ pt
1 kg	2 lb 2 oz	2 lt	$2\frac{1}{2}$ pt

· USEFUL MEASUREMENTS ·

1 level tablespoon (15 ml) contains:

Caster sugar	15 g/$\frac{1}{2}$ oz
Flour	10 g/$\frac{1}{3}$ oz
Salt	20 g/$\frac{2}{3}$ oz
Cocoa powder	10 g/$\frac{1}{3}$ oz
Cornflour, potato flour, baking powder or semolina	7 g/$\frac{1}{4}$ oz
Icing sugar	10 g/$\frac{1}{3}$ oz

There are 3 level teaspoons to 1 level tablespoon

A template or pattern can be made for many of the intricate and fragile, decorative sugar pieces in this book. Both freehand and more structured designs are possible. The pastillage cottage, for example, (far right), when drawn on squared graph paper, can be scaled up or down by means of diagonal lines.

By contrast, the pink flamingo in its lush setting, (below), also made out of pastillage, is a freer design. Similar subjects can be traced from magazines and books, as can the alphabets, opposite. The cottage and the flamingo are illustrated in colour on page 230.

Backdrop 1

Backdrop 2

Foreground

Flamingo

Base

Back of house

Back roof

Front roof

Front of house

Fence   Approx 60 pieces

Fence supports

×4

×4

×4

×4

Base

Chimney

× 2

× 2

Side

Front roof side pieces × 2

Door

Window ledges × 8

Porch
×2

×1

AA ABBCD DEEFF
GHHIIJJKKLLMM
MNNOPPQRRRRST
1234567890
UUVVWWXXYYZ

ABCDEFGHIJKLM
NOPQRSTUVWXYZ
1234567890

ABCDEFGHIJKLMN
OPQRSTUVWXYZ
1234567890

INDEX

· Q ·

· R ·

' Patisserie: An affair of the heart '

MICHEL AND ALBERT ROUX